Contents

THE TECHNOLOGICAL STUDY

Primary School Survey

A Study of
the Teacher's Day

A report by Dr J H Duthie

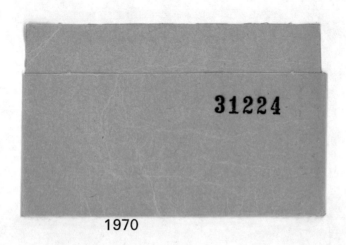

1970

Research Team

Director
J. H. DUTHIE, M.A., Ph.D.,[1]
Lecturer in Educational Psychology,
Moray House College of Education.

Members
MISS A. B. MACDONALD,[2]
Primary School Teacher,
Lanarkshire Education Authority.

MRS. F. M. TAYLOR, B.A., Ph.D.,[3]
Sociologist.

D. J. MACLENNAN, M.A.,[4]
Deputy Head Teacher,
Tillicoultry Primary School.

W. N. C. WARDROP,[5]
Work Study Officer.

[1] Now Senior Lecturer in Educational Psychology, Department of Education, University of Stirling.
[2] Now Adviser in Primary Education, Lanarkshire Education Authority.
[3] Now Lecturer in Sociology, Moray House College of Education.
[4] Now Lecturer in English, Callender Park College of Education.
[5] Now with O. & M. Unit, Welsh Hospital Board.

Consultative Committee

Chairman
G. REITH, M.A., B.Sc., M.Ed., Ph.D., F.E.I.S.,
Director of Education,
Edinburgh Education Authority

Members
D. ASHMEAD, B.Sc., A.R.I.C., M.I.M.C.,
Senior Partner, Urwick, Orr & Partners,
Management Consultants

PROFESSOR R. ILLSLEY, B.A., Ph.D.,
Department of Sociology,
University of Aberdeen

N. L. LAWRIE, B.A., Dip.Math.Stat.,
Senior Lecturer in Operational Research,
University of Strathclyde

MRS. E. C. F. LEGGAT, M.A., Dip.Ed.,
Principal,
Callander Park College of Education

MISS J. M. LOW,
Adviser in Primary Education,
Edinburgh Education Authority

I. McMULLEN, B.A.,
Associate Director,
Resources for Learning Project,
Nuffield Foundation

J. A. D. MICHIE, M.A., M.Ed.,
Director of Education,
Aberdeenshire Education Authority

C. L. MYERS, B.A.,   (*Until April, 1967*)
Local Government Operational Research Unit,
Royal Institute of Public Administration

G. J. POLLOCK, M.A., M.Ed., M.Inst.P.,
Depute Director,
Scottish Council for Research in Education

R. E. RANKIN, M.A.,
Adviser in Primary Education,
Glasgow Education Authority

T. SNEDDON, M.B.E., M.A., F.E.I.S.,
Head Teacher,
Blacklaw Primary School,
Dunfermline

MRS. E. BAY TIDY, O.B.E., N.F.F.T.D.,
Primary Adviser,
Resources for Learning Project,
Nuffield Foundation

B. WHITWORTH, B.A.,   (*From May, 1967*)
Local Government Operational Research Unit,
Royal Institute of Public Administration

Assessors
J. SHANKS,
H.M. Chief Inspector of Schools,
Scottish Education Department

J. G. MORRIS,
H.M. Inspector of Schools,
Scottish Education Department

J. F. McCLELLAN,
Scottish Education Department

W. J. FEARNLEY,
Scottish Education Department

W. A. SMITH,   (*Until September, 1967*)
O. & M. Division,
H.M. Treasury

Secretary
D. STEVENSON,   (*Until March, 1967*)
Scottish Education Department

N. M. KEEGAN,   (*From April, 1967*)
Scottish Education Department

Foreword

By the Consultative Committee

1. Developments in the curriculum and in teaching methods are making more demands upon the teacher's resources and there has emerged an awareness of the need to consider how teachers may be enabled to use their professional skills to the greatest advantage to their pupils. One response has been the growing practice of education authorities to appoint auxiliaries who are not trained teachers. Up to the present the lists of duties assigned to auxiliaries have been drawn up on the basis of collective opinion, and there has been no fundamental examination of duties which do not appear to make demands on the teacher's professional skill. Consideration of this raises questions about the place and function in the class-room of personnel other than teachers, and if this issue is to be adequately examined then it is necessary to make an objective analysis of the teacher's activities which are related to the classroom.

2. The Scottish Education Department was aware that the question of employing auxiliaries applied to all educational establishments, but since it was in the primary school that the most marked changes had taken place, the Department considered that the first attempt at an objective study should be made in the primary classroom. The primary classroom itself presents highly complex relationships involving teacher, pupils, materials and equipment; and a preliminary assessment of the problem indicated that many difficulties would have to be overcome in trying to determine activities at present undertaken by a teacher which could be done by someone else appropriately trained for an auxiliary function.

3. With these considerations in mind the Department decided that it would be desirable if a study could be made which would give education authorities and schools information that would be of help in regard to the employment of auxiliaries at the primary stage. The Nuffield Foundation was known to be contemplating an educational study concerned with the new opportunities presented by developments in educational technology under the title of 'Resources for Learning', and the Department suggested to the Foundation that they should jointly sponsor a research project. The Foundation's Trustees welcomed this venture in partnership and agreed to share the costs.

Appointment of the Committee and the Team

4. In May, 1966, the Scottish Education Department and the Nuffield Foundation appointed a committee to act in a consultative capacity, and to recruit a Director who would lead a research team in an investigation of the scope for the employment of auxiliaries in primary classrooms and prepare a report on the findings. Members of the Committee were appointed having regard to their experience in education, of management and work study techniques and of research. The team was recruited on the footing that there

ix

would be members with practical experience of the classroom, of social science research and of work study methods. Callander Park College of Education provided accommodation and administrative and financial services.

5. At meetings of the Committee and its Sub-Committees, Dr. Duthie, the Team Director, presented papers showing, in the early stages, the plans for research and, in the later stages, the emerging results.

Aspects of the classroom observed in the course of the Survey

6. The Survey broke new ground in that it was based on direct and continuing observation of primary classes which were representative of the country as a whole. It soon became apparent that it could produce a unique store of observations, and it was agreed that while it would not be possible to analyse all of them within the period of this Survey it would be folly not to have them recorded and retained for later analysis, since there was no certainty that a similar opportunity would arise in the near future. Moreover, this information seemed likely to be of value in relation to the 'Resources for Learning' project initiated and sponsored by the Nuffield Foundation. Therefore, although the research was mainly concerned with the scope for using auxiliaries the Director was encouraged to develop his interest in the analysis of teaching and learning and to experiment with ways of describing this process. The results of this additional research include an analysis of pupil/teacher interaction using existing techniques, and an account of techniques devised by the Director with a view to throwing more light on the teaching-learning process.

The scope for auxiliary assistance to teachers

7. The central question was whether there was a place for auxiliaries in the classroom as distinct from auxiliaries who would help with the administrative tasks which have to be discharged in the running of a school. The research establishes on the basis of systematic observation that there is scope for auxiliaries in the classroom; it indicates the kind of work which such auxiliaries might do; and it outlines ways in which their services might be shared in a school.

The value of auxiliaries

8. The Report suggests that if auxiliaries undertook the duties identified in it, over the country as a whole there would be approximately 30 per cent. of classroom time in which auxiliary help could be usefully employed. While the percentage would vary greatly from class to class and from school to school, on the average they could be usefully employed in the ratio of one auxiliary to three teachers. However, this was the first objective analysis of its kind ever undertaken in this country and it was done in classrooms in which there were no auxiliaries. Accordingly, while the Report takes much of the discussion about auxiliaries out of the realm of conjecture it should be regarded not as the last word, but rather as the first stage of an investigation into their use. The next and necessary stage should be further

research based on the outcome of this Survey, including observation of the effect in classrooms of employing auxiliaries trained for the duties specified in the Report; and this view is shared by the Director.

9. The Report estimates that the financial consequence of employing auxiliaries on the ratio of one auxiliary to three teachers could amount to an expenditure of £3m. per annum for the country as a whole. Clearly the high expenditure envisaged requires that educational benefits be obtained, for example, by affording teachers opportunity to give more attention to individual pupils and possibly by the evolvement of forms of school organisation which would enable the professional skills of the teaching staff to be used in a more efficient way. This lends support to our opinion that further experimentation and observation are required. Although it is unlikely that it will be practicable in the immediate future to recruit auxiliaries on the scale suggested in the Report, the number of auxiliaries employed in schools is likely to continue to increase, particularly in those schools where there are special needs. Thus it is important that the further research which we have suggested be carried out quickly so that the nature and extent of the benefits may be assessed and the results made available to provide a source of guidance on ways in which auxiliaries can give the greatest assistance to teachers.

Conclusion

10. Accordingly, we commend the Report to the Secretary of State and the Nuffield Foundation and we recommend that:

(i) the Report should be drawn to the attention of education authorities;

(ii) further research, organised at national level, should be carried out to assess the educational benefits which would accrue from employing auxiliaries trained to undertake duties of the kind defined in the Report; and education authorities employing auxiliaries should be invited to co-operate;

(iii) research should also be undertaken by appropriate agencies on the wider issues in relation to teaching and learning in the classroom which have been opened up by the Director in the later chapters.

CHAPTER I

Introduction

The Consultative Committee, in its Foreword to the Report, has described how the research project came into being, how it has been financed and how a Research Team was appointed.

This introduction provides a general orientation to the research project as a whole: an excerpt from our Remit is followed by a calendar of the events which together formed the project. A few words are then offered in justification of the form which the Report itself takes, followed by a discussion of the problems which we faced at the beginning of the Survey and the general steps which we took to solve them.

The research remit

In its 'Outline of the Projected Study', the Scottish Education Department stated that:

'The aim of the study is to establish the effective scope for relieving teachers by the employment of auxiliary staffs; the range of duties which such staffs might undertake; and the nature of the training which would be appropriate for them. Auxiliary staffs are employed now on a limited scale in a number of schools, but this is being done on an empirical basis only, since no systematic attempts have hitherto been made to determine the duties which such staffs ought to undertake or how they should be trained.

'The study will involve (i) a survey of the teacher's task in the classroom, mainly on the basis of observation in a range of primary schools; and (ii) the preparation, in the light of this survey, of an analysis of the teacher's activities. The study will not be concerned with assessment of the performance of teachers or any attempt at evaluation of the work done in the classroom. It will attempt simply to make an objective analysis of the pattern of the teacher's activities in the school on the basis of systematic observation involving techniques of work study. This has not been done before, and it is likely to prove very useful.

'A study of this kind will illustrate in detail the range of tasks which a fairly substantial sample of teachers have to perform. In particular it will identify activities which do not necessarily require their professional skill and training, and will help in estimating to what extent such activities take up the teacher's time.

'The analysis would be based on observation of the various activities undertaken by the teacher in the course of the school day, ranging from (i) manifestly pedagogic duties such as direct instruction of the class or group or individual and preparation for, and supervision of, class and group activities to (ii) functions which in the ordinary way would not necessarily be regarded as requiring the particular skill of the teacher.'

In the course of their initial discussions, the Consultative Committee and the Research Director interpreted the Remit as indicating that the study should have a dual purpose: the scientific or theoretical one of trying to develop the beginning of a comprehensive theory of instruction (based on the analysis of 'manifestly pedagogic duties'); and the practical or 'technological' purpose of producing data which would make possible the efficient and effective implementation of auxiliary assistance in primary schools.

Calendar of events

The Research Team started its work in September, 1966 and spent the first year in planning and carrying out preliminary observations in schools. The main study took place between September, 1967 and March, 1968. During this period the Team visited, and observed in, a randomly selected and representative sample of all Scottish primary schools. (See Chapter IV.) Analysis of the data and the writing of the Report took place between April and August, 1968.

The shape of this report

A Research Report such as this can be written in at least two ways. One is to present the findings formally and systematically. Such an approach can be concise but it leaves the reader to guess at what really happened. The other approach is to tell the story of the Project from the beginning, as it developed. Although perhaps lacking in elegance, this is the method which has been adopted since we believe that it can give the reader greater insight into the problems which we faced and into the solutions we arrived at.

Taken to extremes, an historical Report could take as long to read as the research took to conduct and clearly we have had to be selective in what we have written. However, we have tried to be selective only in such ways as omitting descriptions of the many blind alleys which we explored and not in selecting only those aspects of the research which, for one reason or another, we wish to make public.

For the reader who wants a quick overall view of the Project, the historical approach may not of course commend itself, and for him there is, in Chapter VII, a formal summary of the technological study together with cross-references to more detailed explanation elsewhere. For the reader who reads the Report in its intended form, this Chapter should provide a summary of the position reached at the end of what has been an intricate exposition of a complex research project.

Initial problems and their solution

We have said that the study has had a dual purpose: a technological purpose and a theoretical one.* For both purposes, it was necessary to undertake an objective analysis of teachers' activities. This is clearly a

---

* These two terms are later used to label and to distinguish the two main parts of the study. For this reason it might be worthwhile to underline the reasons for adopting them. In the 'theoretical' part of the study, what we are trying to do is to develop a 'conceptual framework' for primary school teaching and learning, which may eventually pave the way for a genuine theory of instruction (in the broadest sense of the term 'instruction'). More will be said about this in Chapter X, but enough has probably been said to show why we use the label 'theoretical' to describe this part of the study. The term 'technological' has been adopted to describe that part of the study relating to the employment of auxiliaries in the primary school because our aim here has been the practical one of providing information to enable teachers and administrators to use auxiliaries as effectively as possible. We use the term 'technology' in its accepted sense of 'a systematic body of facts and principles related to a comprehensive practical and useful end'. (English & English, 1958.)

difficult task, not least because the process of education is a complex one. We were faced with the problem of analysing the intricate series of inter-changes between teacher and pupil which, together with unobservable mental events and the context of past events, go to make up the teaching/learning process. More than this, we were faced with classes in which the relative simplicity of formal teaching has been replaced for much of the day by learning situations in which children work independently or in groups, consulting books or the teacher, making decisions, trying out hypotheses. For all of this we were set the task of finding a comprehensive analytical framework, the beginning in fact of a theory of instruction. At the same time, we were faced with the task of solving a particular practical (or 'technological') problem—the employment of auxiliaries in the primary school—within this general context.

We had hoped, when the Survey commenced, to tackle both the theoretical and technological aspects of the study in one comprehensive investigation. Had this been possible, it would have enabled us to provide a systematic theoretical rationale for the technological study. However, the size of such an undertaking, together with the requirement that we produce results for the technological study within two years gradually forced us to separate the two aspects of the investigation and finally to concentrate more and more on the technological study to the exclusion of the theoretical one.

Another factor contributing to this change in emphasis was the lack of previous research in either of these fields. Certainly studies have been made of the classroom situation, and analytical techniques have been developed. We have used one of these—the OScAR technique—in the course of the investigation. But most of these studies are concerned with the analysis and 'cataloguing' of rather superficial features and events. As Medley and Mitzell say of their own work in this field:* 'A principal defect in OScAR [one of the foremost techniques available] is its failure to get at any aspect of classroom behaviour related to pupil achievement of cognitive objectives. The three dimensions that it measures represent what are probably the most obvious differences among classes—how orderly and relaxed they are, in what ways the pupils are grouped, and the general content of the lessons being taught. To measure these reliably was relatively easy; to measure more subtle and crucial differences which OScAR misses will probably be more difficult.'

It was clear, almost from the outset, then, that we could not hope to solve both of our sets of problems—the theoretical and the technological—in one grand experiment. Instead we were gradually forced to divorce the two sets of problems and to approach a solution to each of them by a process of successive refinement. What we did in the case of the technological study was to develop an instrument, based on our initial observations and to try it out in schools, discover its faults and limitations, formulate a new or extended version and try that out. In all, there were three such attempts at refinement. For want of a better term, we have called these successive refinements 'Waves'.†

---

* 'A Handbook of Research on Teaching', edited by N. L. Gage (Page 286).

† The term 'pilot study' was considered inappropriate since this term is usually taken to refer to the experimental work as such, whereas by the term 'Wave' we refer to the whole cycle of observation, analysis, fault-finding and construction of a new or modified instrument. To the best of our knowledge this is the first time that the Wave technique has been used in educational research in Scotland.

The research project, as we have said, consisted of three such Waves by which time we were satisfied that (in the area of potential auxiliary utilisation at any rate) we were obtaining the data which we required. The main experiment as such was then undertaken, and it is on the basis of the data collected at this stage that our final analysis was made.

(This approach has some support from Holt (1950) and Donaldson (1963), who suggest that psychological researchers spend too little time in defining the problem and too much in conducting experiments which are merely elegant.)

We have described how we were faced with the problem of analysing an extremely complex situation with little or no help from previous investigations; how we decided to adopt a research strategy of successive approximations or Waves until we were sure that we could tackle the problem adequately; and how we were gradually forced to divorce the theoretical and technological aspects of the study. We turn now to problems of methodology.

Each aspect of the study—the theoretical and the technological—requires a different method, or set of methods, for its solution. In the case of the former as we have said earlier, we are attempting to develop a comprehensive 'conceptual framework' which we hope will pave the way for a theory of instruction.* Now this is a 'scientific' endeavour in the sense that we are trying to build models of the educational process which can later be tested against reality. (One of the chief differences between this attempt and other attempts such as philosophical ones, is that we are not constructing 'ideal' or 'typical' models but models based on actual classroom observation.) More will be said about this endeavour in Chapter X, but it should be emphasised that we are at the very early stages of observation and theory-construction. At this stage in the theoretical investigation, all that is required in the way of method is direct observation, coupled with model-building.

In the case of the technological part of the study on the other hand we are attempting to provide information which will enable educators—teachers and administrators—to make the best use of auxiliaries. Clearly this is a different kind of enterprise; and yet there are striking resemblances between this and the more 'scientific' study. This study too requires that we clear the ground, that we know what we are talking about before we undertake the investigation proper, and we have tried to clear the ground by the general technique of successive approximation in the form of successive Waves.

In order to define those duties which the auxiliary may take over from the teacher we have had to find what the teacher at present does in the classroom. By systematically describing the teacher's rôle and by identifying those duties which do not require her full professional competence, it has been possible to define what it is that the auxiliary might usefully do.

When we first formulated the task in this way it became clear that there were four possible methods of tackling the technological problem. The first was to ask teachers and head teachers, from their knowledge of teaching, to define the duties for us. If we had confined ourselves to this technique we could by the use of questionnaires have covered all teachers, and head

---

* By 'theory of instruction' is understood a theory which describes the cognitive aspects of the teaching/learning situation.

4

teachers, in Scotland. Unfortunately, much of the information which we required could not be put in questionnaire form—e.g., we required an accurate measure of the time spent on the various duties so that we could make some attempt to calculate the degree of auxiliary implementation likely to be required. A similar criticism can be made of the second possible technique—the interview. However both of these methods have been used in a limited way to supplement information which has been gained more directly by the third possible technique—direct observation.

Observation in the classroom—the technique recommended in our remit—has several advantages over the methods so far described: as we have implied the most important of these is that the data which it produces can be quantified; that is to say that we can specify within certain known limits the time taken by the teacher to perform certain specified duties. In direct observation it is also possible to use a much more refined system of defining duties than we could use in interviews or in questionnaires, where the analytical categories have to some extent to be explained to the participant. (Of course observation has its disadvantages, principally that it is time-consuming and hence cannot be used to cover every primary school in Scotland. However the techniques of sampling, whereby the schools which we do visit can be taken to represent all Scottish primary schools, compensates for this disadvantage.)

The fourth of the possible techniques is to set up an experiment, or series of experiments, in which auxiliaries are actually introduced into the classroom.* In this way it is possible to observe directly the effects of actual implementation, both on the auxiliary's task as we envisage it, and on teaching itself. But first, of course, it is necessary to establish what it is that the auxiliary can do, and as we have said, direct observation of the teacher's task—the technique adopted for this study—appears to be the most appropriate method.

Although considered desirable, it has proved impracticable to incorporate an experimental investigation in the Survey, given our time scale of two years, and it may be considered worthwhile to follow the present observational study with a controlled experiment. Only in this way is it possible to investigate the effects of actually introducing auxiliaries into the classroom.

What we have done in the technological part of the study then is to adopt the technique of systematic direct observation, backed by the limited use of interview and questionnaire in the schools in which observation has taken place in order to establish the duties which an auxiliary might undertake. During the first three Waves, we refined these techniques until they produced the required data in an unambiguous form. Finally, we have used the techniques in the main investigation to collect the information which we require from a representative sample of Scottish primary schools.

The question of what to observe arose at once, of course, and it might be appropriate to make a few comments about the difficulties which we faced in this regard before proceeding.

When we first attempted to write down systematically what happened in a classroom, our first reaction was that the task was impossible. Our next was that we had to select only those aspects which were relevant to the study. In other words, the aims of a study determine what is selected for analysis. In

---

* Two American studies, the Yale–Fairfield (1958) and Bay City (Park, 1956) studies, employed this fourth technique.

the theoretical part of the study these problems were raised in acute form and we shall deal with them in the appropriate section. In the technological part of the study, the problem was less acute but still sufficient to cause us considerable difficulty. Not only was it necessary to define accurately what aspects of classroom activity concerned us: it was also necessary that our observers be able to record these aspects reliably* and on the spot.

The history of the study, which comprises a major part of the Report, records our struggle to come to grips with this problem of what to observe, how to record it, and how to classify what we record. Rather than anticipate, it might be best at this stage to leave the reader with foreknowledge of the difficulties which we faced and to follow us through the various Waves to the solutions which we finally adopted.

Summary of Chapter I

In Chapter I, we have described our remit (pages 1, 2); given an overview of the Survey (page 2); discussed the reasons for the form the Report takes (page 2); and described the problems which we faced when we first started (pages 2, 6). In this last section, we described how it became progressively more necessary to divorce the theoretical and technological parts of the study. We also described how, in the technological study, we decided to approach the design for the final investigation by means of a series of successive approximations or 'Waves'. This course of action was necessitated by the complexity of the situation and by the lack of research literature in the area of auxiliary implementation. We described how, in the course of these successive approximations, we decided to adopt the method of direct observation, backed by the limited use of questionnaire and structured interview, rather than direct experimentation involving the introduction of auxiliaries into a selection of schools.

---

* A further discussion of the reliability of the observations is given in Appendix B.

CHAPTER II

The First and Second Waves

The First Wave: first attempts at systematic description

Our remit required us to look at two components of the teacher's job—at what might be called the 'professional' component, that is to say at the actual task of teaching; and at those duties of the teacher which do not require her full professional competence. As the Survey progressed, these two parts of the study became progressively divorced but as we have said at the beginning we set out with the idea of tackling both problems in a single investigation. Our first attempt at the design for such an investigation, based on our efforts to select appropriate events from the vastly complex series of classroom interchanges, resulted in the following preliminary analysis. (The categories have not survived in this form and are described chiefly for the sake of historical completeness):

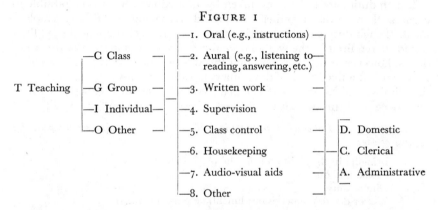

FIGURE I

Even at this stage, there is a partial division into 'teaching' and 'non-teaching' duties, although the inclusion of 'housekeeping' as a sub-division of 'teaching' is indicative of our desire at that time to produce an integrated experimental design. (Domestic, Clerical and Administrative duties should of course be read as sub-divisions of Housekeeping.)

While 'Housekeeping' remains as a category in our final analysis the other distinctions are no longer employed. We also found, in our analysis of the teacher's professional duties, that the sub-divisions of teaching into aural, oral, etc., had to be abandoned. In our first visits to schools, they proved to be useful as categories for *recording* teachers' activities, but trivial when it came to an analysis of the 'meaning' of classroom discourse. Quite apart from the fact that they enabled us to record only the teacher's behaviour and not the children's, an analysis into speaking, listening, etc., tells us little about what the teacher was actually trying to achieve. These preliminary attempts are, in other words, open to the same criticism that has been made of other studies—that they record only the superficial aspects of classroom activity.

Although our preliminary analyses did not survive their first encounter with the classroom, they did provide a starting-point for subsequent classification. It was also clear, in these first days of classroom observation, that the analysis of even the housekeeping duties was a task of considerable magnitude and so for the remainder of our observation during the First Wave, we concentrated on the recording and analysis of those duties alone.

Housekeeping Duties within class hours

Our first approach to the problem of defining potential auxiliary duties in more detail was to list those duties which *prima facie* seem to be the sort which an auxiliary might carry out. (These are of course to be distinguished from those which are clearly educational and which are the responsibility of a trained teacher.) The list of potential auxiliary duties was based on the classroom observation of teachers' activities during our visits to schools and included such items as the following:

Cloakroom duty, issue of dinner tickets, bringing the pupils in from the playground, accompanying children to the library and gym, first aid, maintenance and rehabilitation of equipment, registration. Our first observations produced a list of thirty-two such items.

If such duties are to be undertaken by an auxiliary, it must be possible to organise them so that together they provide reasonably continuous employment. If each duty could be carried out at any time of the school day, little would be required in the way of organisation. On examination of the list of duties, however, it became clear that this was not the case. Some duties have to be done at a fixed time of day; others must occur within certain necessary time-limits; and so on. We developed five such analytical categories which have been used throughout the Survey. These are given in full below:

(1) CATEGORY A *Duties which are* fixed *in the sense that they can only occur at a particular time of day:*

    Bringing in the children from the playground
    Cloakroom duty
    Dinner duty
    Wet or dry day supervision: lunchtime plus interval(s)
    Dispersal
    Lost and found
    Lavatory supervision
    Assisting pupils with clothing
    Accompanying children to physical education, library, etc.
    Accompanying children out of school
    Transporting, setting-up and running audio-visual aids

(2) CATEGORY B *Duties which are* partly fixed *in the sense that they occur within certain necessary time limits:*

    Registration
    Determining milk numbers
    Issue of milk { central / in classroom
    (including any mopping up, collection of empties, etc.)
    Issue of dinner tickets
    Running of 'Tuck Shop' in class
    Distribution and clearing of material in the classroom

8

Collection of dinner money
Savings
Lost and found
Collection and distribution of pupils' work

(3) CATEGORY C *Duties which are non-fixed in the sense that although they are observed to occur at a particular time of day they could be allocated to another occasion.*

Giving out of materials centrally
Objective marking
Keeping in condition of materials (paint, crayons, clay, etc.)
Giving out of travel tickets
Maintenance of audio-visual aids
Ordering of materials for 'Tuck Shop'
Preparation during the school day
Maintenance and rehabilitation of equipment (books, jotters, paint brushes, pencils, etc.)
Collection of dinner money
Savings
Lost and Found
Record Keeping
Writing instructions, assignments on blackboard

(4) CATEGORY D *Duties which occur at times which cannot be predicted and which cannot readily be allocated to other occasions. These duties are directly related to the educational activity of the teacher.*

Distribution and clearing of materials in the classroom
Maintenance and rehabilitation of equipment (e.g., books, jotters, paint brushes, pencils)
Collection and return of pupils' work
Record Keeping
Assisting pupils with clothing
Writing instructions, assignments on blackboard
Accompanying children to physical education, library, etc.
Accompanying children out of school (e.g., visits)
Transporting, running and setting-up of audio-visual aids

(5) CATEGORY E *Duties which occur at times which cannot be predicted, which cannot readily be allocated to other occasions, but which are not directly related to the educational activity of the teacher.*

Accidents and first aid (e.g., cuts, spilled water)
Lost and Found
Lavatory Supervision

Where duties have been classified in more than one category this has been done for one of two reasons: either because we observed that particular duty being handled in more than one way, or because it could easily have been handled in more than one way. Thus the distribution of materials in the classroom may be either a partly-fixed duty (category B) in the sense that it must be done in time for the lesson in question, but could be done at any time before then; or it may belong to category D if the teacher requires that the task be carried out during the actual lesson. Similarly, collection of savings can be organised either as a category B (partly-fixed) duty or as a category C (non-fixed) duty. We have used the former classification when the head teacher has organised the collection of savings in such a way that they must be collected by a certain time (e.g., in order to take the money to the Bank). The latter classification has been used when there is no such restriction.

The duties which we have listed and categorised so far are all related to what might be called 'housekeeping' functions in the school and have been classified as 'Housekeeping Duties: Within Class Hours'*

The Second Wave: the definition of further possible auxiliary duties

In the First Wave we made a start at the problem of defining possible auxiliary duties by describing and categorising those duties about which there could be little or no argument. We did not find it necessary at this stage to define in detail the principles upon which the selection of duties was based other than to classify these as Housekeeping Duties, and to distinguish them broadly from those duties which are clearly the function of a trained teacher.

During First Wave observations, it became clear that there were other duties which were less easily distinguished from the educational process but which nevertheless might be undertaken by an auxiliary. For the adequate definition, classification and allocation of such duties, it was necessary to develop a set of principles which would enable us to distinguish those duties, closely tied up with teaching, from teaching itself. This task occupied us for most of the Second Wave.

Since we had to develop a set of principles for the definition of these more complex duties, it would clearly have been best to await the development of those theoretical aspects of the Survey which are described in Chapter X. We were, however, required to produce results within the two-year span of the Survey and hence this specific analysis had to proceed in parallel with the more general theoretical analysis of teaching. (However, this general theoretical analysis, as it proceeded, did provide a sort of framework for our work in this more specialised area, and hence provided some of the cross-fertilisation which we had hoped for.)

We commenced our analysis of these duties by first of all collecting verbal descriptions of them made during first-hand classroom observation. These descriptions were then discussed by the Team and a list was prepared of those which were considered intuitively acceptable. Attempts were then made to formulate the principles upon which this selection of duties had been made.

The first principle which we adopted was that no duties performed by an auxiliary must involve structuring or restructuring of situations: that is to say that at no point may auxiliaries... 'define and describe relationships present in a situation so that pupils may be aware of them'; nor may they '... set forth data so that relationships may be seen.'†

Two kinds of situation fall within the scope of this principle.

---

* 'Housekeeping Duties: Within Class Hours' are to be distinguished from those which occurred out of normal class hours. Data for the latter (Housekeeping Duties: Outwith Class Hours) had to be collected by questionnaire; data for the former were, of course, collected by direct observation. (For a discussion of unobserved Housekeeping Duties see pages 21–22).

† English and English (1958): 'A Comprehensive Dictionary of Psychological and Psychoanalytical Terms'.

The first may be called, for lack of a better term, 'mechanical situations' and these involve both receptive and communicative behaviour on the part of the auxiliary. The examples given below should help to clarify what is meant by each of these terms.

(1) (a) *Receptive behaviour in mechanical situations—examples:*
(i) general supervision while children are engaged in activities and the teacher is dealing with a small group: here presence of another adult could be beneficial. (See also (1(b)(i) and 2(b)).
(ii) objective marking in the classroom situation.*
(iii) check that children are following their work cards in order. (See also 1(b)(v).)
(iv) keep records of the progress of individual children under the general guidance of the teacher.
(v) general supervision of children working outside the classroom.

(b) *Communicative behaviour in mechanical situations—examples:*
(i) help pupils with minor problems in uses of material—especially in activity groups.
(ii) label drawings, etc., for P.1 children who cannot yet write, i.e., auxiliary writes down what child says.
(iii) answer children's questions about mechanical situations and direct pupils whose questions require explanation to the teacher, i.e., auxiliary acts as buffer between class and teacher who is involved with a group, to avoid unnecessary interruptions and to avoid queueing.
(iv) read out test items for class tests.
(v) help pupil find next assignment card.

The second kind of situation which would appear to fall within the scope of the principle may be called an affective situation, and concerns problems of motivation and class relationships. Again there are two divisions, into auxiliary behaviour which is primarily receptive and auxiliary behaviour which is primarily communicative.

(2) (a) *Receptive behaviour in affective situations—example:*
child brings work for admiration. (Although allocation of this duty to an auxiliary would avoid interruption of the teacher it might be argued that admiration of work involves a bond between teacher and pupil which is important in the creation of interest. Whether the teacher need always be involved in this is probably a matter for argument. In practice we have found that teachers are often so busy that they are unable to give attention to the child.)

(b) *Communicative behaviour in affective situations—example:*
encouragement to children working in groups while teacher works with individuals.

---

* Decisions must of course be made on the basis of the results of objective tests, and the auxiliary would have to be trained to draw the teacher's attention to those cases which required it. She might also be trained to pick out recurrent errors for general treatment by the teacher in the class situation.

It might be argued in the case of some of these items that they provide an opportunity for educational activity which requires a trained teacher and that by using an auxiliary this opportunity would be lost. While this may appear true in certain instances (for example, in item (1)(b)(i)) it is also true that in activity-group teaching the teacher cannot make use of all of these opportunities as they occur so that many of the opportunities are lost in any case. The auxiliary, by her presence, may in fact free the teacher to make more use of these educational situations as they arise.

A fortiori, in the context of 'Housekeeping Duties' (see pages 8–10) the teacher who has been using the collection of dinner-money to give practice in arithmetic would be freed by the employment of an auxiliary to create the best possible educational context for the learning of such skills and would also be free to put to better purpose the time which becomes available when pupils have acquired these skills.

These 'working principles', developed through an analysis of a preliminary list of duties arrived at intuitively after classroom observation, were then used to construct a list of the more 'complex' duties which an auxiliary might carry out. The purpose of these working principles was of course to distinguish between teaching duties on the one hand and those duties which do not require the full professional competence of the teacher on the other. The principles themselves, if fully adequate, would become important components in a theory of instruction. We do not pretend that they have achieved this status but as working principles they have proved extremely useful and have helped us to distinguish reliably among duties in this difficult area.

We were faced with the need to find a general term to describe such duties, and although not fully satisfactory, decided upon 'Supervision' as the term which was most appropriate. In carrying out such duties, the auxiliary in general observes the work which the pupils are carrying out and helps them with those aspects which have to do with the execution rather than with the understanding of the work in question. (The examples which have been given as well as the principles upon which these examples are based, should also help to explain our adoption of the term 'Supervision'.)

First thoughts concerning Housekeeping Duties: Outwith Class Hours

During the Second Wave, as well as developing the Supervision principles which have been described we began to tackle the problem of collecting data concerning those Housekeeping Duties which occurred out of normal class hours.

Clearly not all Housekeeping Duties occur within normal class hours. Many Housekeeping Duties are carried out before school starts, during intervals, after the children have left, and at the teacher's own home. We were of course unable to collect data about the incidence of such duties by direct observation and hence were forced to adopt other techniques. In the course of the Second Wave we compared informally the effectiveness of two techniques of collecting such information: in some cases we collected it by interview with the teacher and in others by the use of a draft questionnaire.*

---

* This questionnaire was restricted in its use to the teachers whose classes we observed. It should not be confused with the more widespread use of a questionnaire—a possibility which was abandoned.

Both techniques have their disadvantages but as a result of our experience in this and the following Wave, we came out in favour of a structured interview, using a check-list which was developed during the early stages of the Third Wave. (See pages 21, 22.)

First thoughts concerning the organisation of the auxiliary's working day

During the Second Wave we also began to explore methods of organising auxiliary duties into a workable day. We examined several possibilities at this stage, most of which proved to be unworkable. However, the basis for a system did begin to emerge. It was clear that, whichever system of organising duties we eventually adopted, it would be necessary for the observer to collect information concerning the starting time for each duty, the time taken and hence information concerning the distribution of potential duties throughout the school day. The observer would also have to analyse the duties into their various categories: Housekeeping: Within Class Hours: A, B, C, D or E;* Housekeeping: Outwith Class Hours; and Supervision. To collect such information systematically, we constructed an analysis sheet at the beginning of the Third Wave. (This is shown on pages 17–20.)

Having collected this information, it was then possible to construct a working day for the auxiliary, based on actual observations in the classroom, in the following way:

(i) Allocate category A duties (fixed) within the classroom day.

(ii) Allocate category B duties (partly-fixed), establishing their specific location in relation to the allocation of fixed duties, and in relation to the limiting times placed on these specific circumstances.

(iii) Allocate category C duties (non-fixed) in a similar way. (These by definition can occur in any gap.)

(iv) Allocate category D duties and Supervision Duties by a process which takes account of their variable nature. (This process was developed during the Third Wave; a full description of it is given in Chapter V.)

Summary of Chapter II

In Chapter II, we have described historically the development of the Survey in its technological aspects, through the first two Waves or successive approximations.

In our discussion of the First Wave, we described the first tentative model of the teaching/learning situation, most of which was later discarded because it was too superficial (pages 7, 8).

The First Wave also included an analysis of those duties which *prima facie* seem to be the sort which might be undertaken by an auxiliary. These were classified as Housekeeping Duties: Within Class Hours. They are subdivided into five groups—'A' duties (fixed); 'B' duties (partly-fixed); 'C' duties (non-fixed); 'D' duties; 'E' duties; and Supervision. (For full definitions of each of these categories and lists of the appropriate duties, see pages 8, 9).

---

* See pages 8, 9.

The Second Wave saw the beginnings of the separation between the theoretical and technological parts of the Study, and the division of the technological study into Housekeeping Duties: Within Class Hours; Housekeeping Duties: Outwith Class Hours; and Supervision Duties. A start was also made in considering possible ways of organising an auxiliary's duties within a working day.

CHAPTER III

The Third Wave

The Third Wave consisted principally of further refinement of the House-keeping and Supervision categories which had been constructed in the Second Wave, and of the development of the techniques to be used in the analysis of the data. It also included a 'dress-rehearsal' for the main investigation.

Further refinement of the categories for the analysis of Supervision Duties

We have described how, during the Second Wave, we had formulated principles which enabled us to say why certain activities were appropriate to an auxiliary whereas others were the province of the professional teacher. At the beginning of the Third Wave we tried to employ these principles as a basis for distinguishing among teacher activities. In doing so, we again observed in classrooms and searched particularly for duties which might qualify as 'Supervision'. On these occasions two observers worked independently in the same classroom, and on their return to base, analysed their data independently, using the principles which have been described. In many cases, the principles did enable the observers to produce identical independent decisions as to which activities were to be classed as 'Supervision' and which as 'Teaching'. In other cases, however, there was considerable disagreement.

In the cases in which disagreement arose among Team members as to which was the appropriate category for a particular activity we first of all had a general discussion among the Team as a whole to see if we could resolve the difficulty on the basis of the principles which have been described. As a result a specific rule was formulated which enabled the Team to agree on the classification of the activity in question. This rule was then entered alphabetically in a 'Rule Book' to be used in similar circumstances in the future (see Appendix A for details).

During the Third Wave this cyclic process of observation, analysis, comparison, discussion and resolution of conflict, followed by entry in the Rule Book, was continued until members of the Team working independently were producing virtually identical analyses of new situations. The result was a set of specific rules, based on the general principles described in the previous chapter, which enabled members of the Team working independently to agree about the amount and kind of auxiliary duties in any class they observed. The rules which the Team adopted, all of them in conformity with the general principles already described, are given in Appendix A.

Once we had reached the stage of virtual agreement on each new set of observations, we checked the level of agreement among Team members statistically. Checks were made on the accuracy with which Team members estimated (1) the time taken for the performance of the duties; (2) the corresponding starting times; and (3) the nature of the duties thus timed (i.e.,

15

whether members of the Team working independently agreed in their identification of the duties they observed).

Details of the data, of the calculations carried out, and of the results of these calculations are given in Appendix B. They indicate that a sufficiently high degree of agreement among observers was achieved.

Recording of Housekeeping and Supervision Duties: data sheets

In the previous section and in Chapter II we described the classification of potential auxiliary work into Housekeeping and Supervision Duties. During classroom observation, the occurrence of these duties was recorded in long-hand by Team members. For the purposes of subsequent analysis, it was necessary to translate these longhand records into a standard format. The format adopted is given below.*

In their longhand records, Team members noted the occurrences of the duties, the length of time the duties took on each occasion, and their distribution throughout the observation day. To facilitate this process of timing, the Team used foolscap sheets, ruled across in minute intervals, giving ten minutes per sheet. During recording, it was thus a simple matter to move down the sheet from section to section as the time passed. The $1\frac{1}{8}$ in. spaces were adequate for all recording purposes. (The high reliabilities achieved in timing indicate that this system is satisfactory.) It was decided to use the minute as the basic recording unit, all times being rounded up or down to the nearest minute. Events of duration of less than half a minute were recorded as 'instances'. The data thus obtained were subsequently analysed and recorded on the data sheets, to which we have already referred (Figs. 2(a) to 2(d)).

GENERAL OBSERVATIONS ON DATA SHEETS

(i) *Layout:* The data sheets were printed on double foolscap and on both sides so that a single sheet represented an observation day.

Information about the school and class was entered under the appropriate headings on the 'morning' side of the sheet.

Each half page was divided into a Housekeeping section and a Supervision section.

For each Housekeeping and Supervision section there was a time-scale; a column for comments (these were intended to provide a cross-reference to the original record and were not for the purposes of analysis); a column in which to enter the length and distribution of duties (see below); a column for the classification of duties; and a common column, centrally located in which the content and organisation of the lesson could be entered.

(ii) *Entries:* Possible auxiliary duties (in either the Housekeeping or the Supervision columns) were entered as instances for duties of under a half-minute's duration; or as timed periods in which the starting and stopping points of the duties were recorded and the intervening period marked by a continuous line. These times were recorded, as we have already stated, to the nearest minute.

---

* See Figs. 2(a) to 2(d). Figs. 2(a) and 2(b) show the morning session of a P1/2 class in a four-teacher school. Figs. 2(c) and 2(d) show the afternoon session of a P5 class in a larger school. (These examples are not intended to be representative.)

Figure 2(A)

School Name		Class	P.1-2
No. of Teachers	4	No. on class roll	39
Total Pupils	133	No. of pupils present	30

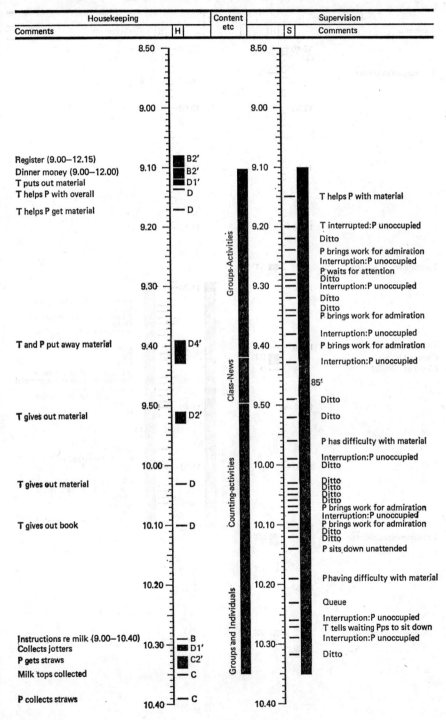

FIGURE 2(B)

Start of School Day	. . 9.00	Lunch Interval . 12.15–1.30
Morning Interval(s)	10.45–11.00	Afternoon Interval . 3.00–3.15

Finish of School Day . . 3.55

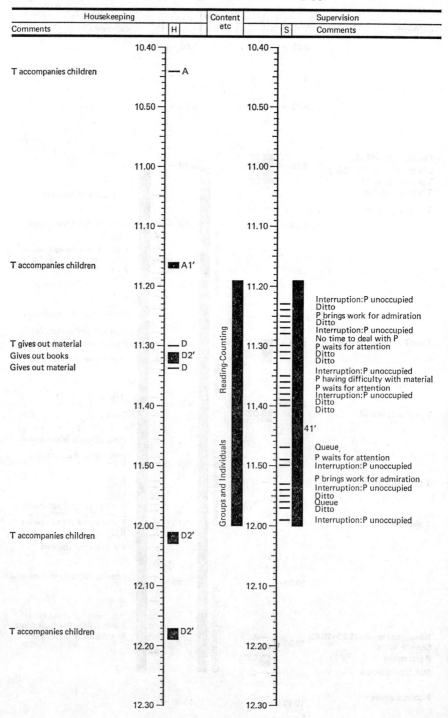

FIGURE 2(c)

(Figs. 2(c) and (d) describe the afternoon session in P5 of a 16 teacher school with 850 pupils. The class roll in P5 was 37; 32 pupils were present on the observation day.)

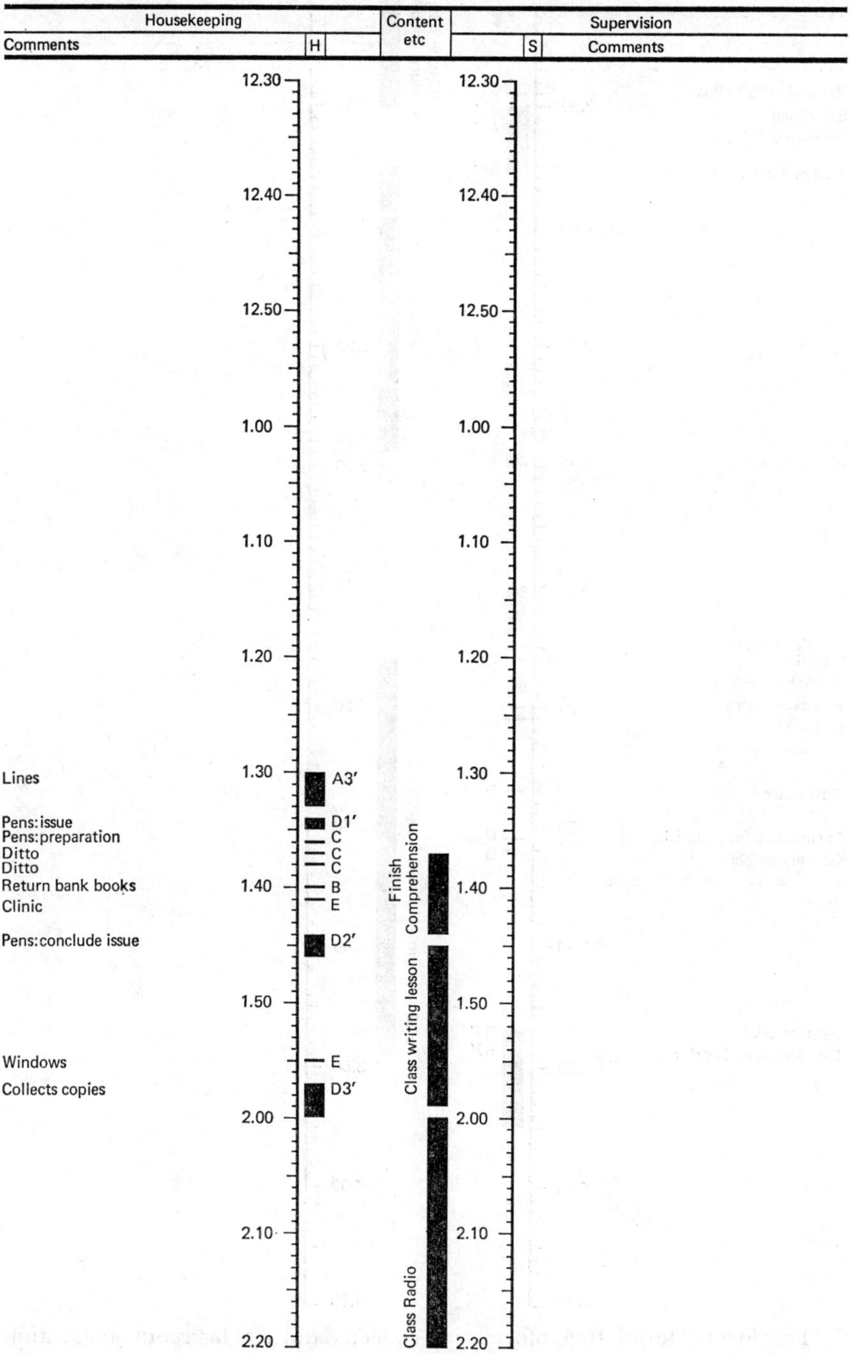

Housekeeping			Content etc		Supervision	
Comments	H			S	Comments	

Time markers (Housekeeping side): 12.30, 12.40, 12.50, 1.00, 1.10, 1.20, 1.30, 1.40, 1.50, 2.00, 2.10, 2.20

Time markers (Supervision side): 12.30, 12.40, 12.50, 1.00, 1.10, 1.20, 1.30, 1.40, 1.50, 2.00, 2.10, 2.20

Housekeeping Comments:
- Lines — A3′ (1.30)
- Pens: issue — D1′
- Pens: preparation — C
- Ditto — C
- Ditto — C
- Return bank books — B (1.40)
- Clinic — E
- Pens: conclude issue — D2′
- Windows — E
- Collects copies — D3′ (2.00)

Content etc:
- Finish Comprehension
- Class writing lesson
- Class Radio

Figure 2(D)

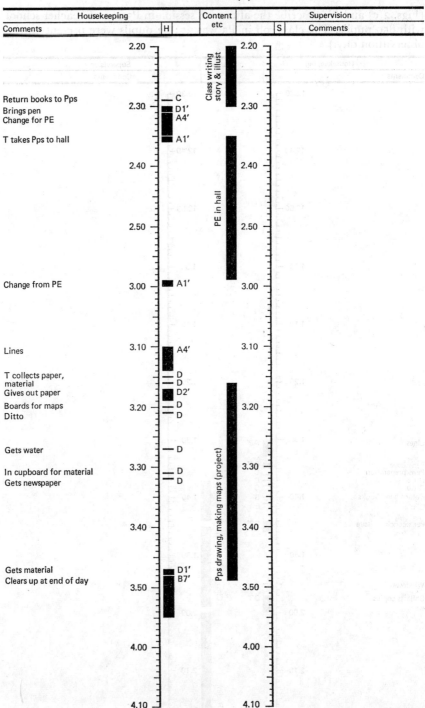

This form of tabulating information collected during classroom observation proved satisfactory for the purposes of the Survey and it was decided to adopt this procedure for the main investigation.

Housekeeping Duties: Outwith Class Hours

We have described, in Chapter II (page 12), how we began to tackle the problem of collecting data for those housekeeping activities of the teacher which occurred *out of normal class hours*: how we compared the effectiveness of two possible techniques—interview and questionnaire—and how we came out in favour of the structured interview. The decision to use a structured interview was finally taken during the Third Wave, and it was at this time also that the check-list for the interview was constructed.

The construction of the check-list was carried out by a process of trial-and-error. We first of all constructed a tentative list of likely duties based on our lists of observed Housekeeping Duties. We then discussed informally with teachers the purposes of the Survey, indicated the kinds of activities in which we were interested, and asked them to describe to us the work which they had carried out in these areas during the past few days. After a number of such interviews we constructed an amended list of such non-observed Housekeeping Duties and attempted to use the list to structure subsequent interviews: that is to say we interviewed teachers about their out-of-class housekeeping activities, basing our question on the list of duties, and asking for estimated times spent on such activities on the previous day. Where teachers volunteered information about duties which were not listed, we added that duty to the list. We hoped, by employing such structured interview techniques, to collect the same kind of information from all teachers about the Housekeeping activities which, for lack of assistance, they have to undertake out of normal class hours. Each of these duties was of course judged to be one which did not require the full professional competence of the teacher and which could be carried out by an auxiliary if one were available.

As a result of our experience in using the check-list during interviews in the Third Wave it was decided to give the teacher a copy of the list to refer to during the discussion. At the end of the discussion, during which the purpose of the list was indicated, we asked teachers to note down times spent on each of the activities during the previous day. (This included Saturday and Sunday where the observation day was a Monday.)

The list used is given below:

'Estimate as accurately as possible in minutes the time spent on the following activities during the previous school day out of class hours (i.e., before and after class hours, during free periods and out of school hours). If the previous school day is a Friday, would you also include work done during Saturday and Sunday:

	Classification
1. Making expendable material (work cards and charts, etc.)	C
2. Correspondence for obtaining project material, audio-visual aids, etc.	C
3. Rehabilitation and maintenance of materials, books, etc.	C
4. Keeping in condition materials (clay, paints, etc.)	C
5. Putting out and clearing of materials	C
6. Control and distribution of material (books, jotters)	C
7. Stock and requisition	C
8. Progress cards, medical cards, report cards	C
9. Marking of objective tests	C
10. Audio-visual aids—obtaining from store, setting up and clearing away	C

11. Servicing mechanical equipment   C
12. Typing   C
13. Duplicating   C
14. Supervision of corridors, stairs, lines, cloakrooms, playgrounds   A
15. Dinner supervision   A
16. Wet day supervision   A
17. Outside escorting   A
18. Selling of biscuits, crisps, etc.   C
19. Any other? Organising parties, plays, parents' evening, exhibitions,
        visits and outings.   probably C

Although these activities were undertaken by the teacher out of normal class hours they would be carried out by the auxiliary during her working day. Furthermore these are of course Housekeeping Duties and for the purposes of calculating potential auxiliary work they should be added to the Housekeeping Duties which were observed by the Team. In order to add these duties to observed Housekeeping Duties, each of them has been classified according to the categories A–E described on pages 8, 9; the appropriate classification is given in the right-hand column of the list above. Since they had no information about the analytical techniques, this column was not included in the version given to teachers.

As might be expected, most of these duties are non-fixed (C) since they occurred out of normal class hours. Item 14 is, however, fixed (A) since, in those cases where such supervision is required, the school time-table dictates the mass-use of corridors, etc. In some schools there are no official times for the use of playgrounds. In such cases, the children use them as and when they please and do not appear to require special supervision. Under these circumstances, teachers have not entered a time for this item.

Item 15, a fixed duty, was treated separately according to the policy of the school, as were items 16 and 17.

In no case was a Housekeeping Duty recorded both here and under the heading 'Housekeeping Duties: Within Class Hours'. Thus if corridor supervision was observed, it was ignored in the check-list.

Information, obtained through structured interview rather than direct observation, must be treated rather more circumspectly than the other data in the study. It might be argued that the teacher, anticipating the presence of observers in her classroom on the following day, might spend more than her usual time in preparation. While this may have been the case, it is likely to be compensated by the fact that she may have spent less time on the actual day in preparation activities because of the presence of the observers. While such a form of compensation is not ideal, no other form of data-collection offered hope of improvement. The Team are of the opinion that in making their estimates of time spent in such duties teachers were both careful and conscientious. Teachers were reassured that zero entries were expected to occur since preparation tends to come in bursts, and some zero returns were, in fact, made.

During the Second and Third Waves, then, we finally completed work on the three sets of categories which were to be used in the main experiment: Housekeeping: Within Class Hours; Housekeeping: Outwith Class Hours; and Supervision. The first two sets of categories are of course designed to collect information about similar activities. The reason for the separate analysis of these activities is that, when they are undertaken by teachers, they occur under different conditions. When undertaken by an auxiliary, the two kinds of Housekeeping activity would be treated identically and the auxiliary would undertake only two major kinds of duty: Housekeeping and Supervision.

The design for the main investigation: sampling

Having completed the construction of our analytical techniques, we next approached the question of the experimental design for the main investigation. The main purpose of the technological study is two-fold: to produce evidence upon which can be based systematic suggestions for the employment of auxiliaries in Scottish primary schools; and to make an estimate of the ratio of auxiliaries to teachers which could be justified on the basis of our observations. To perform these tasks adequately we required first of all to carry out our observations in a sample of primary schools which was representative of all primary schools in Scotland; and secondly to design our investigations in such a way, and so to select techniques of statistical analysis that we could measure where real differences among schools lie. These two issues—sampling and statistical analysis—are related. We deal with the sampling issue first.

Our preliminary observations and discussions had suggested that the important distinguishing characteristics for schools and classes in respect of the incidence of non-teaching activities are:

(a) size of school, and
(b) yearly stage of class.

The simplest way of choosing a sample taking into account these characteristics is a two-stage one involving some form of random selection:*

(a) of particular schools;
(b) of classes within these schools.

In other words, we first of all selected schools at random and having made the selection of schools, selected at random classes within these schools. (Other possible stratification variables were considered. None of these however met the twin requirements of feasibility and relevance. E.g., it would have been useful for us to have stratified our sample according to sociological criteria such as urban—suburban—rural. On enquiry, however, we found that the lack of such information about the 2,610 primary schools in Scotland made such a course of action impracticable.)

---

* Note that in two-stage sampling, where there is a certain selectivity, albeit in a random way of the units for use in the second stage of sampling, there is an increase in the expected error of the overall population estimate in relation to an equivalently sized one-stage sample. (We use 'population' in its statistical sense to refer to all classes in Scottish primary schools.) The justification for the two-stage sampling process chosen for the study is that it is convenient, flexible and easy to control. The results which are derived from it are probably less accurate than those which would have been obtained from a single stage sample of classes—if it had been possible to enumerate the population of these for the whole of Scotland, and had our resources allowed us to visit such a sample.

Details of the two-stage sampling method which we adopted are given below.

(a) STAGE ONE: SELECTION OF SCHOOLS

It was not enough to select schools at random. Given the limitations imposed on the sample size by availability of manpower and time (see page 25), we ran the risk that random selection might omit, or at least under-represent, particular sizes of school. To avoid this danger we grouped or stratified the schools by size,* and ensured that each of these groups was adequately represented in the final sample. (The technique employed is described below.)

Preliminary observations had suggested that the differences in incidence of non-teaching activities among adjacent school sizes are greater in the smaller schools, e.g., the differences between, say, one- and two-class schools appeared to be greater than the difference between fifteen- and sixteen-class schools. We therefore decided to represent school sizes singly at the lower end of the range and to employ increasingly large groups towards the higher end of the range. The actual stratification employed is as follows:

1 class; 2 classes; 3–4 classes; 5–6 classes; 7–9 classes; 10–13 classes; 14+ classes.

(b) STAGE TWO: SELECTION OF CLASSES

Our preliminary observations indicated differences in the incidence of non-teaching activities in the different yearly stages and for reasons similar to those put forward for stratifying schools by size we stratified by yearly stages according to the grouping P.1 and P.2 ('Infants'); P.3 and P.4 ('Juniors'); and P.5, P.6 and P.7 ('Seniors').†

For reasons to do with the analytical techniques employed (see page 26) it was necessary to observe four classes in each school where this was possible. (In smaller schools we visited all classes.) Again, two of these classes had to be from one of our strata and two from another. Thus in one school, we visited two infants classes and two junior, in another, two infants and two senior, and in another, two junior and two senior.

As in the case of selection of schools, selection of classes within strata was also at random where there were more than two classes in a department. Selection of the strata to be used in a particular school was also made at random and allowed for equal representation of each of the strata over the sample as a whole.

---

* School size was measured by number of classes rather than by number of pupils or number of teachers since number of classes gave the least ambiguous measure and in the light of our observations was most closely related to our purposes. Number of teachers, for example, has several possible meanings, depending in part on the area from which the school is drawn —this is true even when part-time teachers are defined in terms of their full-time equivalent— e.g., 'seven teachers' may mean six teachers and a non-teaching head teacher with six classes, or it may mean six teachers and a full-time teaching head teacher with seven classes. In some cases seven-teacher schools have only five classes. Number of classes is on the other hand uniform in its meaning throughout the population and although there are variations in staff utilisation these can if necessary be treated as concomitant variables.

† It must be emphasised that these groupings were used for analytical purposes only: there is no implication that this is necessarily the best way to organise primary education.

(c) THE SIZE OF THE SAMPLE

In determining the size of our sample, we had to consider our resources in terms of manpower and time. One condition of our entering classrooms to observe teacher activities was that the non-teacher member of the Team had to be accompanied by a teacher-member. Because of this it was necessary to divide the Team into two pairs, each pair containing a teacher member.*

Given the need for the development of observation categories through a long process of successive Waves, and the need to provide adequate time for the analysis of the data and the writing of the Report, it was necessary to restrict the period of the main experiment to six months.

The final restriction was the period of time for which it was necessary to observe any one class. Clearly the short answer is: 'the longer, the better'. Experience in the preliminary Waves suggested that one complete day was perhaps the best compromise, provided that we had met the teacher beforehand to reassure her as to our purposes. We felt it necessary to observe a complete day, rather than part of a day, because the day is one of the basic educational units, i.e., in our observations, teachers' requirements for auxiliary help varied more within the day than from one day to the next. (Variations from day to day could be picked up in the analysis since the schedule of school visits (see Appendix G) ensures that each school day is represented equally often.)

The approximate number of classes which we could observe was thus dictated by three factors; the number of pairs of observers available (two); the amount of time available (six months); and the length of time to be spent in each class (one day). Bringing these three factors together and allowing time for travel and for analysis of the data, it was possible for the Team to observe, in the course of the main study, approximately one-hundred-and-twenty classes.

(d) CHARACTERISTICS OF THE SAMPLE

The stratification of schools and of classes, and the number of schools and classes to be sampled for each grouping (see Table 1), are a reasonable compromise between ensuring

(a) that schools of each size are represented in proportion to the total numbers of such schools; and

(b) that there is a similar representation of the number of classes.

The percentage figures for 14+ class schools may appear on inspection to be rather low. The 14+ group however included a sample of *all* schools of this size and above. It is accepted policy that the maximum school size should not exceed fourteen classes† and we may reasonably assume that the percentage of schools in the 14+ group will reduce. Moreover, the sample in this group—as is to be expected from the population curve in which the number of schools falls off very quickly above 14+, includes a majority of schools in the range 14–16 classes. The figures, based on the population data for 14–16

---

* In practice this arrangement suited us well since one member was able to observe activities related to the technological study while the observations of the other member were directed to collecting information for the theoretical study (see Chapter X).

† Primary Education in Scotland, 1965. P. 23.

class schools, are 2·78 per cent for schools (as a percentage of the population) and 0·74 per cent for the classes (as a percentage of the population).

TABLE 1

Size of school (number of classes)	1	2	3–4	5–6	7–9	10–13	14+
Number of schools in sample	7	4	4	3	6	6	7
Number of schools in the sample as a percentage of the total	1·44	0·93	1·01	1·73	1·75	2·12	1·39
Number of classes in sample	7	8	12–16	12	24	24	28
Number of classes in the sample as percentage of the total	1·44	0·93	0·89 / 1·18	1·25	0·91	0·73	0·33

(e) PROCEDURE FOR SELECTING THE SAMPLE

We have described how the sample was a two-stage one in which we first of all selected schools and then classes within these schools. In order to select schools in their appropriate groupings, we first of all numbered all the schools in the population consecutively, as they appeared in the information sheets provided by the Scottish Education Department. We then entered a table of random numbers and selected schools from the population at random until each of the strata given above was complete. Thus if the random number first drawn was, say, 574 and school number 574 was in the two-class grouping, that school was selected and the number of schools available for selection in the two-class category reduced to three. When all schools in a particular category had been selected (e.g., seven in the case of the one-class category), any random number which subsequently fell within that particular grouping was ignored.

Four substitutes were also selected for each of the strata in case any schools opted out for any reason. However, we are glad to be able to report that all schools approached co-operated and that these substitutes proved to be unnecessary.

The next step was to select classes within the schools. Since precise information was not available on a national scale concerning the yearly stage of the classes in the schools selected, we wrote to the Directors of Education concerned once the schools were known. We asked Directors in making their returns to exclude those classes which were not being taken by certificated teachers. (In practice this course of action created none of the sampling problems which we had anticipated—e.g., that we would not have a sufficient number of classes in the required strata.)

The analytical techniques

We have described the instruments which we designed for systematic classroom observation. We have described our sampling design. We turn now to techniques for the analysis of the data. As we have already implied, decisions concerning the design of the statistical analysis were taken at the same time as decisions concerning the sampling design. They are separated in order to simplify the exposition as far as possible.

To be in a position to make well-based suggestions concerning the needs of different kinds of schools (i.e., different school sizes and yearly stages) it is necessary to ensure as far as possible that the differences which occur in the data are real differences rather than differences which might have occurred by chance. For example one might compare infants classes and junior classes with regard to the amount of auxiliary help required and find on the average a difference in favour of, say, infants classes. Before one can take such a difference seriously, it is necessary to show that one would be likely to obtain similar results on a second occasion using a different but equally random sample of such classes. In other words, it is necessary to show that differences in results are statistically significant.

The technique which has been considered appropriate in the present case is Analysis of Variance, a method which not only allows the main variables thought to affect the situation to be compared directly, but also indicates whether they are subject to significant interactions, e.g., whether the measured difference in the amount of auxiliary activity between yearly stages depends on the size of school. (Not only might there be a significant difference between infants and junior classes, but this difference might be affected by the size of the schools in which these classes occur.)

As we have indicated in the discussion on sampling, the statistical analysis was designed to estimate the effect on non-teaching duties of two stratification variables, school size and yearly stage. Because of the nature of the data, a single comprehensive design was impossible: for example although we were able to stratify large schools by yearly stage, it is clearly impossible to do so in the case of small schools. As a result, it was necessary to treat the data by a series of analyses.

The Third Wave pilot study

By the end of the Third Wave we had carried through all the preparation which we, and our statistical advisers, considered necessary for the main investigation. In order to check that everything necessary had been done we tried out our techniques in a limited number of classes using the observational instruments, the experimental design and the analytical tools which we had developed. Since we shall describe in detail the results of the main investigation in later chapters, it is unnecessary to go into the results of the pilot study here.* Suffice it to say that this dress rehearsal confirmed that our plans appeared to be adequate for the task in hand.

Summary of Chapter III

In the course of the Third Wave we completed the process of successive approximation, finalising the form of the instruments and techniques which we had been developing and testing them out in preparation for the main investigation.

The first step was to refine the category Supervision to the level at which Team members, working independently in the same classrooms, produced the same analysis of the duties to be performed by an auxiliary. The reliability of their observations was verified statistically (pages 15, 16).

---

* But see Appendix C, where one aspect of the Pilot Study is described.

We also completed the analysis of those Housekeeping Duties which take place out of normal class hours and constructed a check-list of these duties for use in structured interview (pages 21, 22).

We constructed a sampling design which would represent all Scottish primary schools, discussed the characteristics of the sample in the course of the chapter, and described the technique for drawing the sample (pages 23–26). We described the experimental design in which we employed the technique of Analysis of Variance in order to isolate whatever significant differences exist in the data (pages 26, 27). And finally we described briefly a pilot study which we carried out at the end of the Third Wave in preparation for the main investigation.

CHAPTER IV

Selection of the Schools for the Investigation and Statistical Analyses of the Results

We have described in previous chapters the observational instruments, the sampling design, and the statistical techniques which were developed for use in the main investigation. In the present chapter we first of all describe the actual selection of schools and our initial and subsequent contacts with the schools. There follows a description of the results of our observations and the statistical analyses. The schedule of school visits is given in Appendix G.

The selection of the schools observed

The schools were selected according to the sampling techniques described in Chapter II. Since we undertook not to identify the actual schools which we visited we list only the counties in which these schools are located. This information is sufficient to demonstrate however, that the sampling techniques employed gave good geographical coverage.

Size of school	Geographical area	Classes observed
Seven one-class schools	Shetland	Only one class in school
	Ross and Cromarty	
	Ross and Cromarty	
	Angus	
	Inverness-shire	
	Argyll	
	Ayrshire	
Four two-class schools	Ross and Cromarty	Both classes
	Lanarkshire	
	Lanarkshire	
	Stirlingshire	
Four three-/four-class schools	Sutherland	3 classes
	Perthshire	4 classes
	Orkney	3 classes
	Ayrshire	4 classes
Three five-/six-class schools	Fife	4 classes in each school
	Clackmannanshire	
	Lanarkshire	
Six seven-/nine-class schools	Angus	4 classes in each school
	Angus	
	Lanarkshire	
	Wigtownshire	
	Renfrewshire	
	Berwickshire	

Size of school	Geographical area	Classes observed
Six ten-/thirteen-class schools	Aberdeen City Glasgow Glasgow Glasgow Renfrewshire Angus	4 classes in each school
Seven fourteen-plus class schools	Edinburgh Edinburgh Glasgow Dunbartonshire Dunbartonshire Moray and Nairn Aberdeen City	4 classes in each school

The school visits

(a) PRELIMINARY CORRESPONDENCE

For the main investigation, as for the earlier Waves, the approach to the school was made in two stages. Permission to approach the head teacher of the schools selected was first of all sought from the Directors of Education concerned. Directors were also asked to provide us with information about the yearly stages of the classes in the schools so that we could select the second stage of our sample.

We sent the following letter and informational note to the head teachers with a request that they give a copy of the note to each of the teachers whose classes were to be observed. The letter given below is that for the non-teaching Heads of relatively large schools. Minor variations were made in the letter for the teaching Heads of smaller schools.

(i) *Letter:*

You will have heard from Mr. ...., Director of Education, that the Scottish Primary School Survey Team hopes to visit your school.

I enclose copies of a note which describes the aims and methods of the survey and would add that we have completed our pilot studies and are now embarking on the experiment proper. For this purpose we have selected a stratified random sample of all the primary schools in Scotland in which to carry out our observations. As you will realise it is most important that these observations are made in the schools which have been selected in this random fashion otherwise the data which are produced by the Survey may be biased. For the same reason, classes in such schools must be selected at random. In order to obtain a representative sample of the three departments of the primary school throughout Scotland, it is necessary to select combinations of Infants/Juniors, Juniors/Seniors and Infants/Seniors. The combination selected for your school is Infants/Seniors, using the following classes for observations:

P.1 (Miss A.)
P.2 (Mrs. B.)
P.5 (Miss C.)
P.7 (Mr. D.)

The Team members who hope to visit your school are Miss MacDonald, an Infants' Mistress, Mrs. Taylor, a Sociologist, Mr. Wardrop, A Work Study Officer and Mr. MacLennan, a Deputy Headmaster. They would divide into two pairs and observe each of the four classes for a full day, thus completing their observation in two days. One member of each pair of observers will be a teacher.

The Team proposes to visit your school on .... and .... The four Team members will, however, arrive in the afternoon of .... During the afternoon they would like to have an opportunity for discussion with you. Also, with your permission, each pair of observers would like to meet and talk with teachers whose classes will be observed.

Since we should like to observe classes throughout the complete teaching day, we should like to be stationed in the classrooms about five minutes before the first children enter. It is, of course, important for the purposes of observation that the hours observed are those which normally comprise the school day. I should be grateful, therefore, if you would inform me of your school hours.

If you have any queries concerning the visit I shall be very glad to try to answer them for you. Meanwhile I should like to thank you in anticipation for your co-operation.

(ii) *Informational note:*

Scottish Primary School Survey

The Scottish Education Department, in conjunction with the Nuffield Foundation, has sponsored a survey of primary schools in Scotland. A study of this nature has not been undertaken before and great importance is attached to the survey throughout all its stages. The entire project is under the general control of a Consultative Committee whose membership represents the various interests involved, including the teaching profession, directors of education and colleges of education, together with a number of individuals with experience of survey techniques and research. A team has been appointed to carry out the study over a period of two years. It consists of the research director, two practising primary teachers, a sociologist and a work study officer.

The aims of the study may be described as follows:

(a) to observe teachers' classroom activities in a sample of classes in Scottish primary schools,

(b) to study the relevant organisation of a representative sample of these schools,

(c) to analyse the data collected with a view to isolating those activities which do not require the professional skill and training of a teacher.

In order that the data collected be amenable to statistical analysis schools, and classes in these schools, must be selected on a random basis.

Two Team members, one of whom will be a teacher, will normally spend a day observing the activities that are in progress in each of the classes included in the sample.

Account will be taken of the fact that the presence of observers in a classroom creates an unusual situation. Pilot enquiries, however, suggest that children settle down quickly under these circumstances and it will be appreciated if class teachers do not change their normal classroom routine. Observations will be strictly objective and confidential and will not in any way attempt to assess the work of individual teachers.

A certain amount of time will be allocated to informal discussions with the head teacher, teachers in posts of responsibility, and the class teachers of the classes to be observed. The information obtained in this manner will help the observers to form a comprehensive picture of the school organisation in general.

The Primary School Survey Team and the Consultative Committee very much appreciate your co-operation in this study.

(b) Preliminary visits: details of procedure

Except in one- to three-class schools we carried out preliminary visits to all schools so that we could discuss the Survey and its purposes with the head teacher and the teachers whose classes were to be observed. It can be seen from the schedule of visits (Appendix G) that they usually took place on the day before we were due to observe in that school. It is difficult to over-estimate the value of these visits. They not only served to provide as uniform an observational setting as possible for the subsequent day but also enabled us to establish rapport with the staff of the school.

During the preliminary visit we asked the head teacher about school organisation, using the check-list shown in Appendix F, Fig. 2.* We also asked the head teacher to complete the questionnaire shown in Appendix F, Fig. 1.* In one- to three-class schools each of these lists was filled out during the observation day, either at intervals or after school.

(c) THE OBSERVATION DAY

On observation days, the Team members were at pains to observe the whole of the classroom day. They arrived in the classrooms five minutes before the first children entered and did not leave until the last children had gone.

During observation, they took a longhand record of everything they observed relevant to the Technological Study. This record, of Housekeeping Duties: Within Class Hours and of Supervision Duties, was later transcribed on to data sheets for subsequent analysis. The data sheets are described on pages 16–20. Information concerning Housekeeping: Duties Outwith Class Hours was collected by means of the structured interview described on pages 21, 22. The teacher filled in the check-list (shown on pages 21, 22) after discussion with members of the Team. The completed list was returned at the end of the visit.

In all cases, we experienced full co-operation from the schools we visited. We are glad to be able to say that, wherever we went, we received a warm welcome and often an invitation to return again whenever we pleased.

The results: Housekeeping and Supervision Duties

Table 2, below, provides information about each of the kinds of non-teaching duty recorded by the Team over the whole range of school sizes. To recapitulate, Housekeeping Duties are of five kinds. 'A' duties are fixed and are based on the school as a unit (e.g., Dinner duty is usually done for the whole school).† 'B' duties are partly-fixed and again based on the school (e.g., registration can be so organised that it is done for each class in succession). All other duties are related to the classroom rather than to the school: 'C' duties are non-fixed; 'D' duties related to the ongoing work of the teacher; 'E' duties are 'accidental'; and 'S' refers to Supervision. (More detailed definitions of these terms are to be found on pages 8–10.)

---

* Results obtained will be discussed in a later publication.

† In the table, that the 'A' duties are shown to be different for the various levels, Infants, Junior and Senior, is an artefact of observation and analysis. Although related to the whole school in practice, 'A' duties were recorded in relation to observation based on particular classes. In any one school, 'A' duties would generally be the same for all classes at all levels. (The differences which do exist have been shown to be statistically non-significant.)

TABLE 2

Means (M) and Standard Deviations (S.D.) for various school sizes, levels and duties

(*Times in minutes*)

	'A' Duties		'B' Duties		'C' Duties by Observation		'C' Duties by Interview		Total 'C' Duties		'D' Duties		'E' Duties		Supervision Duties	
	M	s.d.	M	s.d.	M	s.d.	M	s.d.	M	s.d.	M	s.d.	M	s.d.	M	s.d.
School size: 1 *Class*																
Infants ⎫ Junior ⎬ Senior ⎭	16	21	9	8	11	12	64	45	75	50	14	9	4	4	135	56
School size: 2 *Classes*																
lower level	21	1	9	5	6	6	103	53	108	58	20	22	5	7	54	64
higher level	14	15	11	3	12	16	48	52	59	44	16	4	5	4	75	40
School size: 3–4 *Classes and above*																
Infants	22	14	12	7	6	8	69	50	74	53	20	11	9	6	84	51
Junior	16	16	13	11	11	10	61	43	72	45	24	24	7	5	72	56
Senior	17	11	16	12	9	10	77	92	85	93	15	10	8	12	49	52

The data upon which these results are based are more fully reported in Appendix C. Schools with only one or two classes are grouped separately because in these cases it is not possible to make the division into 'Infants', 'Junior' and 'Senior'. For school sizes of 3-class upwards, a series of analyses of variance showed there to be no significant differences in the potential amount of auxiliary work.* It was therefore possible to group these larger size schools together as shown in the Table.

One of the remarkable features of these results is their considerable variability. In many cases, the standard deviation, a measure of the spread of scores, exceeds the value of the mean. This finding indicates that from one classroom and one school to the next there are very large differences in the amount of non-teaching work undertaken or available.

(To some extent we anticipated this degree of variability as a result of the Pilot Study which was carried out during the Third Wave. At that time, however, we were not certain whether the variability was the result of the non-random nature of the sample or whether it was 'real'. If real, we anticipated—probably correctly—that the variability was partly related to variations in the kind of teaching and in methods of classroom organisation, neither of which could be taken into account in the stratification of the sample for the final investigation.)

In Chapter V we shall examine the consequence of this variability for the Survey and for policies related to the implementation of auxiliary assistance in Scottish primary schools. Meanwhile, it should be noted that the only systematic trend which was demonstrated by statistical analysis was in Supervision Duties with regard to yearly stage. As Table VII in Appendix C demonstrates there are statistically significant differences among the Infants, Junior and Senior means for schools of size 3–4 classes and above. Comparing individual means, we find that the difference between Infants and Seniors

---

* Of course it is true that the larger the school, the more auxiliary work there is. The statement indicates only that school size makes no apparent difference to the amount of auxiliary work required in each classroom, i.e., we can safely multiply by the number of classrooms to find the amount of work in any particular size of school (but see safeguards discussed on pages 35, 36).

is significant beyond the five per cent level (a finding which is supported by the analysis of the data from the Third Wave pilot study). Differences between the other pairs do not reach statistical significance. The means are 84 for Infants, 72 for Juniors and 49 for Seniors. In general, therefore, head teachers should expect to find that the younger the class, the greater opportunity is there for Supervision Duties and should take this into account in their planning for the utilisation of auxiliary assistance (see Chapter V).

Summary of Chapter IV

We first of all described the strategy for the main investigation (pages 29–32).

This was followed by a statement of the results of the main investigation in terms of means and standard deviations (averages and spread of scores) (pages 32–34). The variability of the data (i.e., variations in the results from class to class and from school to school) was large. There is, however, a relationship (determined by Analysis of Variance) between Supervision and Yearly Stage of the class: the younger the class, the greater the opportunity for Supervision Duties (as defined in Chapter II). There appears to be no such relationship between Yearly Stage and other auxiliary duties nor is there a relationship between school size and auxiliary duties. (See Table 2 and Appendix C.)

CHAPTER V

A Systematic Review of Certain Policies for the Employment of Auxiliaries

It is clear from the enormous variability of the data that we cannot make specific recommendations for the employment of auxiliaries in particular kinds of schools. Instead, our suggestions must be framed in terms of alternative possibilities, with the advantages and disadvantages, as well as the values inherent in each system, clearly stated. It is for the head teacher to select, and if necessary to adapt within the framework of his Education Authority's policy with regard to the employment of auxiliaries, the system which is most appropriate to his local conditions. Further, the statements which follow concerning implementation possibilities are based on observation of classes and schools the majority of which do not as yet have auxiliary assistance; as a result, these statements have the status of hypotheses—hypotheses based on the best available evidence certainly, but hypotheses nevertheless. This is to say that we are attempting to predict the most appropriate system of auxiliary assistance and the required level of that assistance, based on the schools as they are. We cannot, by the nature of things, and in the course of a two-year survey, say how the situation will change as a result of the employment of auxiliaries nor can we fully assess the exact effect of these various factors involved. On the other hand, as a result of our systematic observations—observations based on a random and representative sample of all Scottish primary schools—we can estimate requirements and possibilities objectively; a system based purely on experience and intuition could not.

We have pointed to the variability of the data and to the effects of this variability on possible recommendations. The variability of the data, however, must be seen in the context of the considerable amount of work which there is for auxiliaries to do, and hence in the context of the ratio of auxiliaries to teachers which on the average is justifiable on the basis of the data.

The ratio of auxiliaries to teachers for which there is an opportunity on the basis of the data

In order to estimate the ratio of auxiliaries to teachers* for which there is an opportunity on the basis of the investigation we have to sum the means for the various duties given in Table 2. This, however, is not a simple process. Apart from the fact that the variability of the estimated duties will increase as means are added, there is also the important problem of conflicting duties: although the duties which the Team observed could not

---

* Strictly, the ratio of auxiliary to classes rather than to teachers since our calculations are based on the classroom as a unit.

clash since they occurred in sequence in individual classrooms, as soon as we expect an auxiliary to undertake duties for more than one classroom,* there occurs the possibility of a clash among duties. This possibility becomes critical in the case of Supervision duties. It will be recalled that these duties are related to the work of the teacher and that they occur at times which cannot be predicted. If we envisage an auxiliary as responsible for carrying out work for two or more teachers, and all teachers want to have supervisory assistance, then it is possible that the times during which they require such assistance may overlap. Policies for avoiding such clashes are given below. Meanwhile in assessing the required ratio of auxiliaries to teachers we assume the worst possible case—that all duties which may clash do in fact clash. Hence our estimate of the justifiable ratio of auxiliaries to teachers is a minimum one. If the various policies to avoid clashes are even marginally successful, then the justifiable ratio will increase.

The ratios are derived from the data on Table 2 as follows. For one-class schools, the means for 'A', 'B', Total 'C' and Supervision are added.† Since these means refer to one-class schools, no clashes can occur and this addition is legitimate.

In the case of two-class schools (and larger schools) no simple addition is possible. Since 'A' duties are carried out for the school as a whole, we include 'A' duties derived from the observation of only one of the classes. The location of 'B' and 'C' duties can be modified (by definition) and hence these duties can be organised so that they do not clash. 'B' and 'C' duties can therefore be treated additively: in other words, for two-class schools we can add the means for 'B' and 'C' work available on the average for two-class schools. In order to avoid a possible clash of duties, and for the reasons already given, we use the Supervision requirements for only one of the classes. (Since only one of the required Supervision periods is allocated to the auxiliary, it is legitimate to assume that this would be the longest of those available.)

The same procedure is followed in the case of schools of three, classes and larger, i.e., 'A' duties and Supervision Duties are included for only one class; 'B' and 'C' duties are treated additively.

On the assumption that an auxiliary will work a six-hour day, the ratio of auxiliaries to teachers for which there is an opportunity on this basis in the larger schools is 1 : 3. In the two-teacher schools there is on the average 4 hours 44 minutes of auxiliary work to be carried out—a little over the 1 : 3 ratio; and in one-teacher schools there is 3 hours 55 minutes—a ratio of approximately 2 : 3.

If auxiliary duties were restricted to 'A', 'B' and 'C' duties (i.e., to house-keeping) a ratio of one auxiliary to every four teachers on the average over the country as a whole would be justified.

Thus although the variability of the data prevents us from making specific recommendations for kinds of school, we are clearly safe in saying that, at a minimum, and accepting the basis for these figures described in the earlier

---

* A requirement which, for economic reasons, will become a necessity. Even a 1 : 3 ratio of auxiliaries to teachers would require the employment of 6,080 auxiliaries (calculating part-time auxiliaries in terms of their full-time equivalent) at an annual cost in salaries of approximately £3,040,000 assuming an arbitrary annual salary of £500.

† 'D' and 'E' duties are omitted from these calculations for the reasons given on pages 39, 40.

chapters of this Report, there is enough work for at least one auxiliary to every three teachers over the country as a whole.

Policies by which the auxiliary's work might be carried out

Given that, even on a conservative estimate, there is a considerable amount of potential auxiliary work in primary schools, the question then arises as to how the auxiliary's work might best be organised. As we have said, the purpose of this and succeeding sections of the Report is not to make specific recommendations for particular kinds of school but to provide models which should help head teachers solve their own particular problems of auxiliary implementation most effectively.

We have defined four policies for the organisation of the auxiliary's work. The first of these has been called an 'On Call' policy, the second a 'Flexible Timetable' policy, the third a 'Fixed Timetable' policy and the fourth a 'Sharing' policy.

By an 'On Call' policy we mean that the auxiliary would be located at a central source and that any teacher who required her services could call her at any time. This is a queuing situation and under this policy it would be a case of 'first come, first served'.

By a 'Flexible Timetable' policy, we mean that the auxiliary would be allocated to a specific teacher at a specific time. If the teacher concerned does not require assistance for the duty or duties specified then the auxiliary would be free to help other teachers.

In the case of the 'Fixed Timetable' policy the auxiliary is again allocated to a specific teacher (or duty) at a specific time but in this case no re-allocation is possible.

By a 'Sharing' policy we mean that an auxiliary would be allocated to a group of teachers who among themselves and perhaps in consultation with the auxiliary, would decide how the auxiliary should be employed for the succeeding period (e.g., day or week). This policy would throw a greater burden on the teachers who would require to organise their work in colla-boration. On the other hand, if this could be achieved, it might facilitate the sort of collaborative efforts which the Team observed on their visits to some English primary schools (see page 49). Care would have to be taken that the auxiliary did not herself have to resolve conflicting requirements among members of the teaching staff. (It is, we believe, most important that auxiliaries experience adequate job-satisfaction, not least in order that auxiliary staff of sufficient quality remain available.)

The policies in relation to the duties to be performed

These then are the policies. We can arrange them in a table to show which policies are appropriate to each of the duties. Where no entry is made the duty could not be carried out in this way; '(X)' indicates a possible but unlikely solution; and 'X' indicates an appropriate solution.

The fact that Supervision can be carried out by any of the policies does not mean that all policies are likely to prove equally effective for Supervision. Similar considerations apply to each of the duties:

TABLE 3

Duties	A	B	C by observation	C by interview	D	E	Supervision
Unit or Location	School (For all classes together)	School (Classes in sequence)	Central source or Classroom	Central source or Classroom	Classroom	Classroom	Classroom
POLICIES On call	—	—	(X)	(X)	X	X	X
Flexible time-table	—	—	X	X	X	X	X
Fixed time-table	X	X	X	X	X	X	X
Shared	(X)	(X)	X	X	X	X	X

'A' DUTIES

'A' duties, as we have said, relate to the school as a unit and by definition must be done at fixed times. Thus if the school has a policy of bringing in the children from the playground in 'lines'* this duty must be undertaken at a particular time and for the whole school. The simplest way of having this or any other 'A' duty done is to have the auxiliary carry it out on the basis of a Fixed Timetable. No other duties must be given precedence at these times and the simplest way to avoid conflicting requirements is to give each teacher a list of the occasions on which the auxiliary is employed on such duties.

'B' DUTIES

'B' duties must be done within a specified interval. The auxiliary could be left to carry out the duties at a convenient time within the interval, but this might lead to conflict of authority if she were instructed to carry out another duty by a teacher which lasted for the whole of the specified interval. It is probably better therefore to carry out 'B' duties by a Fixed Timetable.

'C' DUTIES

Although by definition 'C' duties are non-fixed, they must of course be completed in time for the lesson for which they are intended. This consideration is central in the discussion which follows.

'C' duties are probably best carried out on the basis of a Flexible Timetable policy. Such a policy, the reader will recall, implies that teacher X will have period P allocated to her for such duties and that if she does not require the auxiliary for this purpose the auxiliary carries out other work either for teacher X or for other teachers. (For a more detailed statement of priorities see page 46). This policy meets the above requirement in that teachers can be sure of getting 'C' duties done at certain times and thus for certain lessons if they want them. It also has the advantage over Fixed Timetabling that the teacher may get extra 'C' duties carried out if the auxiliary is not required by another teacher.† The same is true of a Sharing policy although there is

---

* Not all schools do this. And in some which do, the duty necessarily involves the whole school staff (because of stairs, etc.). In such cases, it would not be possible to have the duty undertaken by an auxiliary.

† Under these conditions, the auxiliary would be instructed to inform the teacher beforehand if the extra work were unlikely to be carried out in time so that the teacher would do it for herself or change her plans.

greater danger of unintentional squeezing out of 'C' duties by, say, Supervision Duties in this scheme. An On Call policy is clearly unnecessary for 'C' duties since by definition they can be carried out at any time. (If the duties *are* related to the teaching situation and must be done at a specific time they are classified as 'D' duties and are treated under the appropriate heading.)

'C' duties then are probably best handled by a Flexible Timetabling policy or failing that by a Fixed Timetable, although the latter would be less economical. 'C' duties could be handled by a Sharing policy but only if all other duties (except perhaps 'A' and 'B') were handled in the same way.

'C' duties, whether on Fixed Timetable or Flexible Timetable policy, must be placed in the timetable with reference to 'D' duty and Supervision requirements; that is to say that, since 'D' and Supervision requirements tend to occur predominantly in the morning 'C' duties will be allocated to afternoons when 'D' and Supervision Duties are less likely to occur. (Of the Supervision blocks which were required by the data in the surveyed schools, 142 occurred in the morning and only 44 in the afternoon. Even allowing for differences in length of morning and afternoon, this is a clear difference in favour of the morning. Within the morning, the majority of requirements fall between interval and lunchtime—the most appropriate time from the point of view of other duties such as registration. Generally speaking then, 'C' duties can be carried out in the afternoon in preparation for the following day's work.)

'D' DUTIES AND SUPERVISION DUTIES

'D' duties are classified along with Supervision since, on examination of the data, 'D' duties do not occur in sufficient numbers to make it worth estimating for them separately. (The Team attempted to 'block' 'D' duties on the same basis as for Supervision so that the duties might be undertaken by an auxiliary and in only a very few cases did blocks of 'D' duties result.)* Only those 'D' duties occurring 'end on' to a Supervision block, or during an actual Supervision block, could therefore be handled by an auxiliary.

Supervision (and concomitant 'D' duties) can be handled by any of the policies. An On Call policy provides maximum flexibility, makes good use of an auxiliary's time, but requires some system of intercommunication.† A Flexible Timetable policy gives almost as much flexibility, makes good use of an auxiliary's time and requires some degree of intercommunication.† In addition a Flexible Timetable prevents the delays and disappointments that are inherent in an On Call system. A Fixed Timetable policy is easy to operate but inflexible in application, making poor use of an auxiliary's time. Finally, the Sharing policy, as we have said, gives a greater responsibility to the teachers who would require to organise their work in collaboration.

Supervision then might appropriately be handled by a Flexible Timetable, an On Call policy or by a Sharing policy. Whether a Sharing policy is adopted is, as we have implied, a general matter, involving questions of relationships and organisation. The choice between a Flexible Timetable and an On Call system is considered at greater length in Appendix E, where the On Call system is analysed in some detail. The conclusions of this analysis and comparison are as follows:

---

* For a discussion of Supervision blocks, see Appendix A, page 84.

† In both cases discussion in the staff room at intervals would probably provide adequate intercommunication.

(1) The On Call system results in a lower level of service to teachers and a lower utilisation of the auxiliary's time for Supervision than a Flexible Timetable policy. It should, however, make auxiliaries available to teachers more frequently, at times when these auxiliaries are actually required.

(2) When the demand for auxiliary's time is considerably greater than the supply (as is likely to be the case in the earlier stages of the service) most requests for service would not be met and it would seem clearly better to adopt a Flexible Timetable in order to avoid frustration.

(3) In general the case for an On Call system, although defensible, is not clearly stronger than that for a Flexible Timetable. Under conditions where most calls for assistance could be met it might be decided to adopt the On Call policy for Supervision because of its slightly greater flexibility. Under normal conditions, the final choice is likely to be between a Sharing policy and a Flexible Timetable policy where Supervision Duties are concerned.

'E' DUTIES

'E' duties occur so infrequently (see Table 2) and last such a short time that they are probably best dealt with by the class teacher unless the auxiliary is already in the room for another reason. Exceptions to this rule would be emergencies and situations involving a teaching head teacher. In the latter case, for example, interruptions for the telephone might well be taken off his hands by an auxiliary.

Summarising the conclusions reached in the course of this discussion it would appear that 'A' and 'B' duties are best carried out by a Fixed Timetable system, irrespective of the policies by which other duties are carried out; that 'C' duties are best carried out by a Flexible Timetable system, provided that the times are distributed in relation to 'A', 'B' and Supervision requirements; and that the policy appropriate to Supervision (including 'D' duties) should be selected by the head teacher from the following policies: Flexible Timetable, Shared and On Call. The On Call policy is unlikely to prove satisfactory except under ideal conditions. For most planning purposes, 'E' duties should be ignored.

A technique for the organisation of the auxiliary's working week

In this section, we are concerned to demonstrate a method which head teachers might adopt to organise the work of auxiliaries as they are appointed to their staff. The basic procedure consists in constructing 'simulated' days by distributing the duties required of the auxiliary along a time-scale graduated in hours to represent the school day. The entries in these simulated days are based on the observations of the Team in the field: content of duties is based on what was most frequently observed, location on the most frequent times of occurrence, and duration upon the average durations observed. The first two variables were specified by examination of the original data sheets. The durations were based on the means contained in Table 2.

In any particular instance the head teacher will not be able to use the data produced by the Survey except perhaps as a first approximation. The data are too variable to be applied in any specific case. The actual content, location on the school timetable, and duration of these duties will depend on the policy of the head teacher and staff, and on conditions prevailing in the specific school for which the timetable is being designed. (In actual practice, furthermore, only an approximate estimate of duration will be possible: the auxiliary would be instructed to fill in any spare time with 'C' duties. Subsequent adjustment of the duration of duties would be necessary in the light of experience.)

A simulated day (or simulated week if day-to-day requirements differ) is built up for the whole school by the process shown in Figures 3(a)–(c). Figure 3(c) shows the full simulated day. Figures 3(a) and 3(b) show the procedure by which the simulated day is built up.

The particular example shown here is constructed on the assumption that a one-to-three ratio of auxiliaries to teachers obtains, and, for the sake of simplicity of illustration, that this is a three-teacher school.

'A' duties are first of all distributed along the time scale (see Fig. 3(a)). These duties are fixed by definition and hence there should be no problem in deciding their location and duration according to the requirements of the particular school.

We have fixed the location of the common 'A' duties with reference to our observation sheets.

Their duration is based on the mean values occurring in Table 2. 'A' duties occur for the school as a whole, hence only a single entry is necessary in the simulated day for each of these duties (compare this with the calculation of 'B' and 'C' duties where entries have to be made for each of the classes). Since the time taken for 'A' duties is likely to be that of the largest class, we base our estimates for 'A' duties on the largest mean in the 'A' column for three-teacher schools, 22 minutes. This period of 22 minutes is then split up among the 'A' duties distributed in Figure 3(a) so that together the 'A' duties for the whole school total 22 minutes.

'B' duties—partly-fixed duties such as registration—are allocated next. Here the procedure differs from the procedure for 'A' duties in that 'B' duties have to be carried out for each class in turn. The values obtained from the 'B' column of Table 2 have to be related to the number of classes in the school—here, three—in order to obtain the durations of the simulated day. To obtain the best estimate of the duration of 'B' duties, we take the average of the entries in the 'B' column. The average value, $13\frac{2}{3}$, is multiplied by the number of classes, three, to give the total time to be devoted to 'B' duties in the school as a whole (41 minutes). Since the Analysis of Variance indicated that there are no significant differences among Infants, Junior and Senior classes with regard to 'B' duties, these are distributed equally among the classes in the simulation.

The location of 'B' duties is of course less critical than the location of 'A' duties since by definition, 'B' duties are partly-fixed, i.e., their location can be determined within certain limits. Clearly 'B' duties must be located in such a way that they do not clash with 'A' duties, and in such a way that they leave maximum gaps for 'C' and Supervision Duties. Their location and duration have been determined in Figure 3(a) taking these requirements into account.

'C' duties chiefly relate to the preparation work to be used by teachers in the classroom at a future date. These are non-fixed duties and as we have said are probably best handled by a Flexible Timetable (i.e., if teacher X does not require help, the auxiliary can help teacher Y).

The duration of 'C' duties is based on the mean of the values in column C (Total), Table 2, as in the case of 'B' duties. Not all 'C' duty requirements can be satisfied on the basis of a 1 : 3 ratio (see overleaf) and since

FIGURE 3

(a) Distribution of of 'A' and 'B' duties (morning)	(b) Addition of 'C' duties to 'A' and 'B' (morning)	(c) Addition of Supervision duties to 'A', 'B' and 'C' (morning)

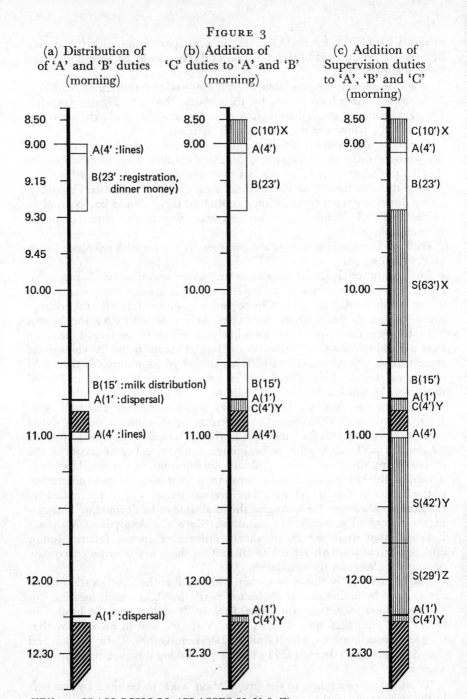

KEY: 3 CLASS SCHOOL (CLASSES X, Y & Z).
RATIO: 1 : 3.

- ▢ : duties carried out on a Fixed Timetable.
- ▥ : duties carried out on a Flexible Timetable, or using an On Call policy, or by a Sharing policy. (In the last two cases, ignore X and Y allocations).
- ▨ : auxiliary's intervals and lunch hour.

NOTE: Labels are attached in Fig. 3(a) to indicate duties which were common to the majority of schools observed.

FIGURE 3 (contd.)

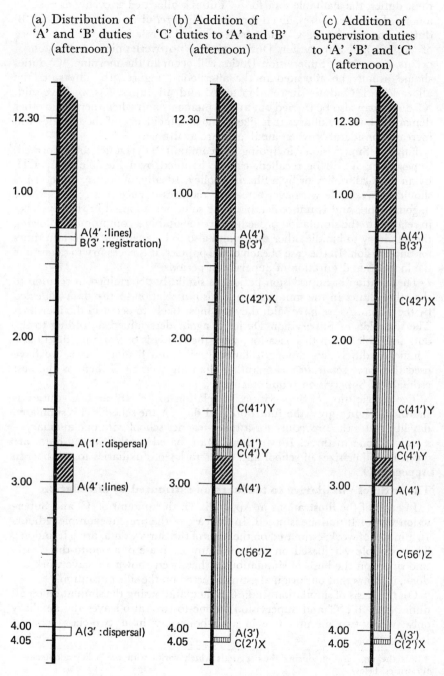

(a) Distribution of 'A' and 'B' duties (afternoon)

(b) Addition of 'C' duties to 'A' and 'B' (afternoon)

(c) Addition of Supervision duties to 'A' ,'B' and 'C' (afternoon)

43

there are no established significant differences among classes with regard to these duties, the available time for 'C' duties is allocated as evenly as possible among the three classes, given the timetabling requirements for 'A' and 'B' duties. The location of 'C' duties is determined in relation to the occurrence of 'A', 'B' and Supervision Duties, so that no overlapping (or 'clashing') occurs. Since most Supervision Duties will occur in the morning, 'C' duties should usually be allocated to the afternoons. Figure 3(b) illustrates the allocation of 'C' duties in relation to 'A' and 'B' duties. (As we have said, 'C' duties can also be carried out at odd moments and when there is no other demand for the auxiliary. It is likely that the incidence of these duties will increase considerably when auxiliaries are available.)

Finally, Supervision (including concomitant 'D') Duties are allocated. Supervision, it will be recalled, can be handled by a Flexible Timetable, by an On Call policy or by a Sharing policy. Ideally, of course, Supervision should be available whenever a teacher requires it since it is related to her ongoing work and is unpredictable. The solutions adopted in these policies in relation to the simulation procedure are inevitably a compromise, allowing the auxiliary to handle other duties and also to be available at certain times for Supervision. In the case of each of the policies, it is necessary to determine the location and duration of Supervision periods.*

The location of Supervision periods is similarly determined in relation to the other duties in the simulation and also in relation to the data collected by the Team. As we have said, they are most likely to occur in the morning. The duration of Supervision Duties is again determined according to the data in Table 2. On this occasion, since the Analysis of Variance did isolate significant differences among Infants, Junior and Senior classes, we have used the three separate means rather than an average of them as the best estimate of Supervision requirements.

The distribution of Supervision, in relation to 'A', 'B' and 'C' duties, is shown in Figure 3(c), the full simulated day for the school. This simulated day illustrates the procedure for a three-teacher school with one auxiliary—a ratio of one to three. Illustrations, again based on the Survey data, are given for other sizes of school and other ratios of auxiliaries to teachers in Appendix D.

The ratio of auxiliaries to teachers as estimated by simulation

In each of the illustrations in Appendix D, the amount of 'C' and Supervision work left undone is noted. In the case of the present example, 2 hours 19 minutes of work, estimated on the basis of the Survey data, are left undone. This example was based on our minimum estimate of a one-to-three ratio and since, on the basis of simulation† it has been shown to leave work undone, it shows that our original estimate erred on the side of caution.

On the basis of simulation studies, in fact, and basing the simulation on all duties ('A', 'B', 'C' and Supervision), a one-to-two ratio leaves the auxiliary only twenty-two minutes free in a six-hour day in a two-class school.‡ (see Figure 4).

* It is the organisation during these periods which varies with the policy adopted—see 'Priorities' below.
† Simulation was necessary to show that the duties could be arranged without clashing.
‡ It should be noted, moreover, that these 'free' times are in a sense artificial: we have, as the result of our policy on minimum estimates, deliberately omitted allocating time for the auxiliary to move from place to place and from task to task.

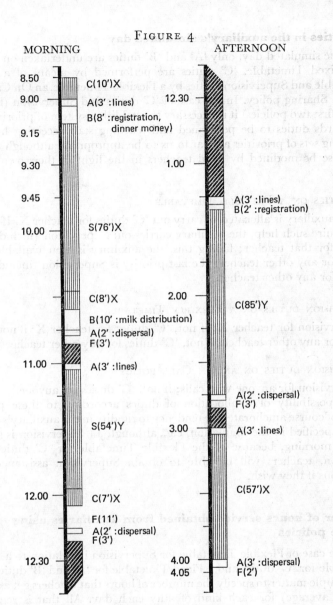

FIGURE 4

MORNING   AFTERNOON

8.50 — C(10')X

9.00 — A(3' :lines)   12.30 —

B(8' :registration,
         dinner money)

9.15 —

9.30 —   1.00 —

9.45 —   A(3' :lines)
               B(2' :registration)

10.00 — S(76')X

C(8')X   2.00 —

B(10' :milk distribution)   C(85')Y
A(2' :dispersal)
F(3')

11.00 — A(3' :lines)

               A(2' :dispersal)
               F(3')

S(54')Y   3.00 — A(3' :lines)

12.00 — C(7')X   C(57')X

F(11')
A(2' :dispersal)
F(3')

12.30 —   4.00 — A(3' :dispersal)
            4.05 — F(2')

KEY: 2 CLASS SCHOOL (CLASSES X and Y).
       RATIO 1:2.

[ ]   : duties carried out on a Fixed Timetable.

[▥]   : duties carried out on a Flexible Timetable, or using an On Call
          policy, or by a Sharing policy. (In these last two cases, ignore the
          X and Y allocations).

[▨]   : auxiliary's intervals and lunch hour.

F   : free time available to the auxiliary on this basis.

NOTE: the atypical distribution of Supervision time is likely to be the result of the small
         sample of two-class schools. In practice and taking into account the general results
         it is likely that the Supervision requirements for younger classes will exceed those
         for older classes.

Priorities in the auxiliary's simulated day

In the simulated day, only 'A' and 'B' duties are undertaken on the basis of a Fixed Timetable. 'C' duties are performed by means of a Flexible Timetable and Supervision Duties by a Flexible Timetable, an On Call policy or by a Sharing policy. In the case of 'C' duties and Supervision (the latter on the first two policies) it is necessary to establish a system of priorities, both as regards duties to be performed and teaching staff receiving help. The following sets of priorities appear to us to be appropriate although they can of course be modified by head teachers in the light of their own circumstances.

'C' DUTIES ON A FLEXIBLE TIMETABLE

The auxiliary is allocated to carry out 'C' duties for teacher X. If she does not require such help, the auxiliary carries out Supervision (including 'D') Duties for that teacher; failing this, the auxiliary is then available for 'C' duties for any other teacher; the last priority is Supervision (including 'D') Duties for any other teacher.

SUPERVISION DUTIES ON A FLEXIBLE TIMETABLE

Supervision for teacher X; if not, 'C' duties for teacher X; if not, Supervision for any other teacher; if not, 'C' duties for any other teacher.

SUPERVISION DUTIES ON AN ON CALL POLICY

Supervision for anyone who calls; if not, 'C' duties for anyone.

The possibility of re-allocation of duties according to these priorities should of course ameliorate any tendency to rigidity in the auxiliary's working day as specified in the simulation, e.g., although all Supervision is specified for the morning, because of the Flexible Timetable for 'C' duties in the afternoon, teachers will be able to obtain Supervision assistance in the afternoons if they wish.

Number of hours service obtained from auxiliaries using these policies

In the case of Flexible Timetable for Supervision in relation to a Flexible Timetable for 'C' duties and a Fixed Timetable for 'A' and 'B' duties, it is a fairly simple matter to specify the number of hours that teachers get assistance (on the average) for each kind of duty each day. All that is required is simple addition. In our example in Figure 3, for example, each teacher receives $13\frac{2}{3}$ minutes of 'B' duties; for 'C' duties, teacher X receives 54 minutes, teacher Y, 53 minutes and teacher Z, 56 minutes; for Supervision, the teachers receive $126\frac{2}{3}$ minutes, $104\frac{2}{3}$ minutes and $106\frac{2}{3}$ minutes respectively.* The total working day for the auxiliary is 6 hours. (The variations in 'C' duties are the result of circumstances; those in Supervision result from differential requirements.)

---

* In practice of course, the auxiliary's day could hardly be planned with such precision: fractions of a minute are mentioned here only to allow the auxiliary's day to add up to six hours. Furthermore, as we implied on page 44 time would have to be allowed in practice to enable auxiliaries to get from place to place.

In the case of the more complex On Call system for Supervision it is also possible to estimate the amount of assistance which teachers would obtain from auxiliaries and this has been done in Appendix E.

Notes on the organisation of the work of several auxiliaries within a single school

We have described in this section how the various duties, carried out by different policies, might be organised into a working week. Before we conclude, however, it should be pointed out that it is possible to organise three of the policies—On Call, Flexible Timetable and Fixed Timetable— in such a way that each auxiliary would serve all classes, or in such a way that each auxiliary would serve only a group of the classes in a school.* For example, if there are five auxiliaries and, say, twenty classes in a school, then all five auxiliaries could serve all twenty classes; or each auxiliary could serve a group of four classes. The merit of the first system is economy: if an auxiliary is absent, all classes can still be served, albeit at a lower rate of service. The merit of the second system is that the auxiliary would come to know the particular pupils and teachers better. A compromise, whereby the second system is normally adopted but reallocation is possible in the case of absence, may provide the best solution.

In relation to this discussion, it should be noted that in larger schools with several auxiliaries it would probably be better for all auxiliaries to undertake all duties. In such circumstances there could be a rota whereby one auxiliary undertook duties such as registration on one week, a second auxiliary on the second week and so on. Alternatively, 'A' and 'B' duties could be divided up so that one auxiliary always took lines, another registration and so on. We are concerned only to avoid a hierarchy of auxiliaries in which some are Housekeeping auxiliaries and others Supervision auxiliaries.

The number of auxiliary personnel required on a one-to-three ratio

Because it would be necessary to employ some auxiliaries on a part-time basis if a particular ratio is to be adopted, we cannot obtain an estimate of the auxiliary personnel required over the country as a whole simply by dividing the number of teachers in the country by the figure three. Taking into account part-time as well as full-time auxiliary staff, the number of auxiliaries required, based on a figure of 18,241 teachers, is 7,127.

Summary of Chapter V

Perhaps the most important result of the investigation is that there is an opportunity for a considerable amount of auxiliary assistance even on a minimum estimate. The ratio is at least one auxiliary to every three teachers (pages 35–37) over the country as a whole and the requirement would be likely to increase for example as teachers learn to make full use of auxiliaries, especially as regards preparation of materials (i.e., 'C' duties).

With regard to the implementation of auxiliary assistance, we have suggested that 'A' and 'B' duties should be carried out on a Fixed Timetable;

---

* This alternative should not be confused with the 'Sharing' policy described earlier.

that 'C' duties should be carried out on a Flexible Timetable (i.e., the auxiliary should be time-tabled to assist one teacher but should that teacher not require her, then the auxiliary should be available to other teachers); and that Supervision (including concomitant 'D' duties) should be carried out by a Flexible Timetable, by a Sharing policy, or perhaps—and only under ideal conditions—by an On Call policy (pages 37–40). Methods of organising the auxiliary's working day are described using the technique of 'simulation' (pages 40–47). Auxiliaries (except under a Sharing policy) may be organised to serve all teachers or a group of teachers (page 47).

Finally, we deal with several issues related to the employment of auxiliaries in schools, including priorities when employing Flexible Timetables and On Call policies (page 46), the number of hours service obtained with different policies (page 46), and the number of personnel required (page 47).

CHAPTER VI

Qualifications and Training Required for Auxiliary Assistants

We can do no more in this chapter than make suggestions based on the duties which we have outlined in the Report, on our reading of the relevant sections of previous reports (e.g., the Yale-Fairfield Study), and on our assessment of other variables such as 'market conditions'.

Entry qualifications

It is notoriously difficult to specify the qualities required for a particular profession or job other than in the most general terms. As a result, refuge is often taken in demanding formal entry qualifications which specify, much more precisely than is justified, the requirements for a particular occupation. It would be a pity if such a course of action were to be taken in this instance since there is probably a large number of potential candidates who would make excellent auxiliaries but who lack formal qualification. (We visited a special school which had a number of highly competent auxiliaries who fell into this category: headmistress and teaching staff were very satisfied with them. The same is true of primary schools we visited in England. In spite of their lack of formal qualifications, auxiliaries and staff worked in close co-operation both in and out of the classroom). This is not to say that a course of training is inappropriate to qualify them for the job. Indeed we would argue that training is not only desirable but necessary in view of the speed of change in educational methods. But entry to training should rest on some other basis than, say, a specified number of 'O' grades. Formal qualifications of this sort should not of course be undervalued, but neither should we ignore candidates who lack them.*

It has been suggested by the Plowden Committee that '... qualities of character, personality and interest' should be '... identified through a study of the candidate's previous record and by interview'. While not excluding these means of assessment we suggest that they be supplemented by the potentially more reliable instrument of a specially constructed objective test. While this might tend to favour candidates with successful school experience it would nevertheless be fairer than past examination results and more reliable than interview. This test would include items which measure the candidate's general educational level as well as such variables as personality and aptitude. Care would have to be taken that the test-items are related to what is required of auxiliaries in schools and that the test does not become a meaningless hurdle which would-be auxiliaries have to jump.

---

* In the final analysis, of course, Education Authorities are responsible for deciding entry qualifications: we must emphasise that these are only suggestions, albeit suggestions based on observation and analysis.

Recruitment and Training

Married women whose children have grown-up ('the motherly sort') are often considered to be most suited to auxiliary work. While we should by no means wish to exclude such candidates, we hope that younger candidates–those who come straight from school to the training course—will also be considered. There are several reasons for saying this: the auxiliary as she is envisaged in this Report, will have a much wider range of duties than 'mothering': and more important, staff to whom we have spoken believe that the teacher should be older than the auxiliary, so that there should be no danger of a conflict of authority. It is clearly easier for a teacher to be in full control of an auxiliary younger than herself than of one who is considerably her senior. Recruitment will of course be affected by demands for workers in other sectors of the economy in relation to the wage offered, conditions of service and attractiveness of the occupation. The job itself, and conditions of service, will probably be considered to be relatively attractive. The wage which is at present being offered by some local authorities—£8 per week—attracts large numbers of applicants. (There were 500 replies to an advertisement inserted by a Local Authority in 1968. 54 appointments were made and a further one in three of the 154 interviewees were appointed to the reserve list.) It is likely, however, that after a course of training auxiliaries would expect to earn a higher salary than this. Furthermore, we envisage that auxiliaries would carry out more highly skilled functions than the majority of those at present in service.

If auxiliaries are to undertake such duties, it would seem appropriate that training courses should not only incorporate extensive practical work, but should also include seminars and lectures on the aims and methods of primary education, child development, and in the skills which are required of an auxiliary. These range from the purely practical skills such as registration and the operation and maintenance of audio-visual aids to the more complex interpersonal skills required for Supervision duties.

A course of this scope would probably require a two-year period of training. Candidates of 21 years of age and over might however be permitted to qualify after a shorter period. Part-time training might be provided for mature candidates with other responsibilities.

CHAPTER VII

Summary of the Technological Study

The Survey consists of a technological study, of its by-products and of a theoretical study. This chapter provides a summary of the technological study which has been described in Chapters I to VI. The by-products of the technological study are described in Chapters VIII and IX and the theoretical study in Chapter X.

The purpose of the technological study

The chief purpose of the technological study has been '... to establish the effective scope for relieving teachers by the employment of auxiliary staffs; the range of duties which such staffs might undertake; and the nature of the training which would be appropriate for them.' (See Research Remit on page 1).

Method and results

Our first task was to specify the duties which were deemed appropriate for auxiliary personnel (see paragraph 1, below). We then observed a representative sample of Scottish primary school classrooms in order to discover the extent to which such potential auxiliary duties at present take up teachers' time (paragraph 2). Having submitted the data to statistical analysis in order to determine whether schools differed significantly in these respects (paragraph 3) we finally examined the feasibility of employing auxiliaries in the primary school (paragraph 4). We take each of these points in turn:

1. THE SPECIFICATION OF POTENTIAL AUXILIARY DUTIES

Potential auxiliary duties have been divided into two kinds: (a) those which can be considered *prima facie* to be the sort which auxiliaries might undertake, and (b) those which require some other, more analytical, justification for their inclusion as auxiliary duties.

(a) *Housekeeping Duties*

The duties which were considered to be *prima facie* of the sort which auxiliaries might undertake have been termed 'Housekeeping Duties' since they comprise those duties which have to do with the day to day running of the non-educational aspects of the school.

For the purposes of the investigation Housekeeping Duties have themselves been classified in two ways—there are (i) those duties which occur within normal class hours (e.g., registration) and (ii) those which occur outwith normal class hours (e.g., the preparation of materials which the teacher may at present carry out at home). From the point of view of work with auxiliaries, there is no real difference between the two kinds of duty; when we come to collect information about the execution of such duties, however, we find that while data concerning Housekeeping: Within Class Hours can be gathered by direct classroom observation, it is necessary to use less direct techniques such as questionnaire and interview to collect data about House-keeping: Outwith Class Hours. Two kinds of Housekeeping Duty, then, are distinguished but only for the purposes of investigation and analysis: both would be undertaken by an auxiliary within normal school hours.

(i) *Housekeeping Duties: Within Class Hours*. A provisional list of Housekeeping Duties: Within Class Hours was drawn up in consultation with members of the teaching profession and Her Majesty's Inspectorate. We then observed in classrooms and modified and added to the list according to our observations. This amended list formed the basis for discussions which led to the final list of duties to be used in the main investigation. Examples of duties from the final list are: Cloakroom duty, issue of dinner tickets, maintenance of audio-visual aids, accompanying children to the library or to physical education and dealing with accidents.

So that we might later organise the duties into a working week for auxiliaries, these Housekeeping Duties were grouped into five categories: *Category A:* fixed duties, which must occur at a particular time of day and at no other (e.g., cloakroom duty); *Category B:* duties which are partly-fixed in the sense that they occur within certain time limits (e.g., issue of dinner tickets); *Category C:* duties which are non-fixed in the sense that although they are observed to occur at a particular time of day they could be allocated to another occasion (e.g., maintenance of audio-visual aids); *Category D:* duties which occur at times which cannot be predicted and which cannot readily be allocated to other occasions. Such duties are directly related to the educational activity of the teacher (e.g., accompanying pupils to physical education where the teacher has suddenly decided to do this. This category would also apply in the case of an unexpected outing, related to what the teacher and pupils had been doing in the classroom.) *Category E:* duties which occur at times which cannot be predicted, which cannot be allocated to other occasions, but which are not directly related to the educational activity of the teacher (e.g., accidents and first aid).

Lists of these Housekeeping Duties: Within Class Hours, grouped according to their five categories, are given on pages 8, 9.

(ii) *Housekeeping Duties: Outwith Normal Class Hours.* Lists of Housekeeping Duties: Outwith Normal Class Hours were drawn up, based on our experience of defining observable Housekeeping Duties. In general, these are concerned with the non-educational aspects of 'preparation'. After a similar process of trial and error we drew up a check-list of such duties, to be filled in by teachers during the main investigation. Examples are: duplicating, putting out and clearing of materials, and correspondence related to the purchase of materials. A full list of these duties is given on pages 21, 22.

(b) *Supervision Duties*

During our preliminary observations, we began the process of isolating those duties which could not simply be delegated to auxiliaries on a *prima facie* basis but which nevertheless might appropriately be undertaken by an auxiliary. Before such duties can be delegated, it is necessary to distinguish between teaching and non-teaching duties. Principles and rules which enable such distinctions to be made were drawn up on the basis of our preliminary observations and are given on pages 10, 11 and in Appendix A. The most important of these principles and rules is that nothing the auxiliary does should involve 'structuring' (see Glossary). Examples of duties which might be delegated on this basis, and which help to explain why we chose the name 'Supervision' for them are: checking that the pupils are following their work cards in order; general supervision while pupils are engaged in activities and the teacher is dealing with a small group; and helping pupils with minor problems in the uses of material.

Thus we collected information on the following kinds of duty: House-keeping Duties: Within Class Hours; Housekeeping Duties: Outwith Normal Class Hours; and Supervision Duties.

2. The main investigation

Having specified those duties which might be undertaken by an auxiliary and categorised them, we then observed a representative sample of Scottish primary school classes (page 23 ff) and recorded the frequency, times of occurrence and duration of each of these duties. Means and standard deviations are given in Table 2, page 33.

3. Statistical analysis of the data from the main study

The data were submitted to Analysis of Variance to test for any significant differences which might exist among school sizes and yearly stages—our two stratification variables. The variability of the data is such that differences appear to exist only in Supervision Duties with regard to Yearly Stage—the younger the class the more opportunity is there for assistance of this kind (pages 32 ff).

4. Technological analysis of the data

Having established that, with the above exception, there were no significant differences with regard to school size or yearly stage, we examined, on the basis of the data, the feasibility of employing auxiliaries in primary schools (Chapter V).

(a) On an average over the country as a whole, and taking an absolutely minimum estimate, there appears to be an opportunity for employing a ratio of one auxiliary to every three teachers. Even if Supervision is entirely ignored, a minimum ratio of one auxiliary to every four teachers appears appropriate. Assuming that the policies for planning an auxiliary's day make it possible to avoid clashes, the ratio of auxiliaries to teachers increases to one auxiliary to every two teachers.

(b) We described four policies for the employment of auxiliaries and related each of these policies to the duties which were to be carried out. The four policies are:

(i) *On Call:* the auxiliary would be located at a central source and any teacher who required her services could call her at any time. This is a queueing situation and under this policy it would be a case of 'first come, first served'.

(ii) *Flexible Timetable:* the auxiliary would be allocated to a specific teacher at a specific time. If the teacher concerned does not require assistance for the duty or duties specified then the auxiliary would be free to help other teachers.

(iii) *Fixed Timetable:* the auxiliary would again be allocated to a specific teacher (or duty) at a specific time but in this case no reallocation would be possible.

(iv) *Sharing:* the auxiliary would be allocated to a group of teachers who among themselves and perhaps in consultation with the auxiliary would decide how the auxiliary would be employed for the succeeding period (e.g., day or week).

On the basis of our observations and analysis it is suggested that 'A' and 'B' duties be carried out by a Fixed Timetable and that 'C' and Supervision Duties be undertaken on the basis of a Flexible Timetable. 'D' and 'E' duties should be ignored unless occurring when an auxiliary is present. As regards Supervision Duties, the On Call and Sharing policies may provide alternatives to the Flexible Timetable policy under certain conditions. Under ideal conditions, the case for an On Call policy, although defensible, is however not clearly stronger than that for a Flexible Timetable; and Sharing implies an educational viewpoint which is rather different from that required by the other policies.

(c) Specimen working weeks for various sizes of school and ratios of auxiliaries to teachers are given in Appendix D. A technique which head teachers could use for the organisation of the auxiliary's working week is described on pages 40–44.

5. QUALIFICATIONS AND TRAINING

Suggestions are given for the qualifications and training of auxiliaries in Chapter VI. It is suggested that, on the basis of our observations of auxiliaries in service, formal qualifications should not necessarily be looked for. On the other hand, there should be an aptitude test and a course of training.

CHAPTER VIII

Further Results of the Investigation: the Availability and use made of Audio-Visual Aids

During their interviews with head teachers the Team collected information about the availability to the school of audio-visual aids (television, tape recorder, film strip projector, sound ciné-projector, record player and radio). During their interviews with teachers, the Team asked them to complete the following questionnaire estimating the use which they had made of each instrument during the past week:

Audio-visual aids   *Mins.*

Estimate as accurately as possible the time spent using the following audio-visual aids during the past *week* Monday to Friday.

1. T.V.   _____
2. Tape recorder   _____
3. Film strip projector   _____
4. Sound projector   _____
5. Record player   _____
6. Radio   _____
7. Other   _____

The following tables summarise the findings:

TABLE 4
Availability and use made of audio-visual aids

Instrument	Percentage of schools in which instrument is available	Percentage use *where available* (see note 1)
Television	67·6%	108·0% (see note 2)
Tape recorder	62·2%	39·1%
Film strip projector	75·7%	39·3%
Sound projector	43·2%	25·0%
Record player	83·8%	48·4%
Radio	94·6%	97·1% (see note 2)

Notes:

(1) The column '*Percentage use where available*' indicates the percentage of those classes which have instruments available making use of those instruments on at least one occasion during the week previous to the observation day E.g., 39·1 per cent of those classes having access to a tape recorder actually used it at least once during the previous week.

(2) Teachers' personal sets were used in a few of the schools, hence the television entry is greater than the 100 per cent of official sets.

(3) Although generally available to the class in question, the instruments may not always have been available when the teacher required them.

(4) Radio and television are used much more than other audio-visual aids, presumably because, although less under the control of the teacher, they require less setting-up. Teachers might make greater use of the other audio-visual aids if an auxiliary were available to set them up, to order films, etc.

TABLE 5

Proportion of time in one week allotted to the use of audio-visual aids

Instrument	1-class schools	2-class schools		3–4-class schools and above			
		Lower	Upper	Infants	Junior	Senior	All stages (IJS)
		Size of school and yearly stage (where appropriate)					
Television	3·3%	3·3%	2·5%	0·8%	1·0%	2·8%	1·5%
Tape recorder	0%	0%	2·6%	0·1%	0%	0·4%	0·2%
Film strip projector	0%	0·7%	1·6%	0·6%	0·2%	0·5%	0·4%
Sound projector	N/A	0%	0%	0·9%	0·2%	0·2%	0·4%
Record player	1·9%	0·5%	0·7%	0·5%	0·2%	0·2%	0·3%
Radio	4·1%	1·1%	2·3%	1·5%	1·7%	1·8%	1·7%
Totals (all instruments)	9·3%	5·6%	9·7%	4·4%	3·3%	5·9%	4·5%

Notes:

(1) Caution should be exercised in interpreting the data for 1- and 2-class schools because of the size of the sample at these levels.

(2) Figures are given to one decimal place because of the small entries in some cells.

CHAPTER IX

The Analysis of Classroom Discourse by means of the OScAR Technique*

It will be recalled that, during their visits to schools, the Team observed in pairs. One member of each pair collected information for the technological study whilst the other collected information for the theoretical study. Since the theoretical study was purely exploratory we decided to utilise the opportunity of observing a random sample of Scottish primary classes by employing also an established instrument for classroom observation. For this purpose we used what was probably the best available technique—OScAR 4V. (Medley, Impelletteri & Smith, 1966). The member of the pair who was collecting information for the theoretical study accordingly employed the OScAR technique on two occasions during the observation day: for a five-minute period in the morning and for a further five-minute period in the afternoon.

The instrument is illustrated in Figure 5. All boxes and capsules to the left of the vertical line are used for recording teacher statements and teacher initiated interchanges. The boxes and capsules to the right are used for pupil statements and pupil-initiated interchanges. Boxes are used for recording statements, capsules for interchanges. Teacher statements may be rebuking, directing, informing, considering, describing or problem-structuring. All pupil statements are recorded in the box to the right and are not differentiated since the instrument is designed chiefly for discriminating among teacher statements and interchanges.

The three teacher capsules are for divergent interchanges, elaborating interchanges and convergent interchanges. Entries within the capsules show how the teacher reacted to the pupil's reply to her statement or question—e.g., by Supporting it (SP), Approving it (AP), Acknowledging (AC), Not Evaluating it (NE), Neutrally Rejecting it (NR) or by Critically Rejecting it (CR).

Medley gives definitions for each of these categories; all definitions necessary for an understanding of the results are given below.

Some caution should be exercised in interpreting the results. Norms have not yet been established for this purpose. On the other hand, since these results are themselves based on a representative sample of Scottish primary school classrooms, they may be used as preliminary norms for this country. At the same time it is possible to interpret the results in terms of the numbers of given occurrences during a specified period and this we have done below. These interpretations give some idea of the patterning of activities in classrooms. Comparisons among Infants, Junior and Senior in many cases indicate trends which we were intuitively aware of as observers and the general impression of the Team is that these figures provide, in objective form, reasonably accurate measures of the patterns of teacher and pupil verbal behaviour in the classes observed.

---

* (Observation Schedule and Record).

FIGURE 5

Observation Schedule and Record Form 4 (Verbal)

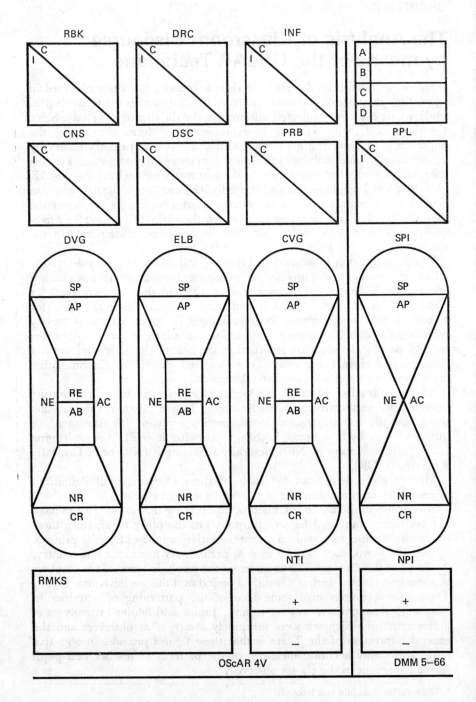

Table 6 gives the total number of entries for each of the boxes and capsules. Thus there were on the average, 3·8 instances of problem structuring by the teacher in ten minutes of observation in Infants classes, 5·5 such instances in Junior classes and 4·4 in Senior classes. 'Problem-structuring statements pose issues, questions or problems about substantive content without giving solutions to them' (Medley, Impelletteri & Smith, 1966, p. 8).

Categories in Table 6 for which there appears to be a trend are as follows: *Rebuking:* approximately twice as frequent in Junior as in Infants and Senior classes; *Directing* (orders or commands): falls off for Senior pupils; *Informing* (facts, principles and ideas): increases linearly with age of class; *Considering:* ('Statements reflecting affection or concern for pupils or their needs, desires, feelings ...') falls off with age. (There is no clear trend for *Describing:* ('a Describing statement is one which merely tells what the class, the teacher, or a pupil has done, is doing, or will do, without pressuring students to behave in a certain way'), although teachers do a lot of it (5 instances in 10 minutes on the average). *Pupil statements* (pupils addressing each other as an integral part of the lesson) should be compared with the remainder of the statements, since the others are all made by the teacher. For an analysis of pupil statements addressed to the teacher, see SPI below).

TABLE 6

Mean frequency and range of frequencies for all categories of OScAR 4V, based on two observation periods totalling 10 minutes. (Means per class for Infants, Junior and Senior).

CATEGORY	Mean Frequency (based on two observation periods of five minutes each)				Range		
	Infants	Junior	Senior	Infants, Junior and Senior	Infants	Junior	Senior
Statements:							
RBK (Rebuking)	3·3	6·1	3·2	4·0	0–6	0–12	0–8
DRC (Directing)	7·7	8·6	5·2	7·2	0–12	0–10	0–9
INF (Informing)	2·3	3·7	4·4	3·3	0–7	0–10	0–12
CNS (Considering)	2·6	2·0	1·0	2·0	0–10	0–11	0–4
DSC (Describing)	5·6	4·0	5·0	5·0	0–8	0–7	0–17
PRB (Problem Structuring)	3·8	5·5	4·4	4·4	0–8	0–20	0–16
PPL (Pupil Statements)	0·4	0·0	0·0	0·2	0–3	0	0
Interchanges:							
DVG (Divergent)	1·6	1·3	1·7	1·6	0–6	0–11	0–22
ELB (Elaborating)	0·7	1·0	0·6	0·8	0–5	0–4	0–5
CVG (Convergent)	7·6	8·0	6·4	7·3	0–25	0–22	0–18
SPI (Substantive— pupil initiated interchange)	2·7	2·9	2·9	2·8	0–7	0–7	0–7

The first three interchanges are teacher-initiated. *Divergent* interchanges relate to questions by the teacher which are 'open-ended'—i.e., there is no one correct answer. In a *Convergent* interchange only one answer is acceptable. *Elaborating* interchanges show the extent to which the lesson 'hangs together'. Here '... the question the teacher asks refers directly to a pupil response immediately preceding it, asking the pupil to discuss, correct or enlarge upon it' (ibid). There is no clear trend with age of pupil. A comparison of the three categories however shows that Convergent questions are much more common than the others. (Further and more sophisticated comparisons among categories are given below.)

A breakdown of these interchanges in terms of the way in which the teacher dealt with the pupil's response to her questions is given in Table 7. Most responses are Acknowledged. The extreme positive end of the continuum (Supported) is used more frequently than the extreme negative end (Critically Rejected).

TABLE 7

ENTRY	EXIT	Mean Frequency (based on two observation periods of five minutes each)				Range		
		Infants	Junior	Senior	Infants, Junior and Senior	Infants	Junior	Senior
DIVERGENT	Supported (SP)	0·2	0·1	0·1	0·1	0–2	0–1	0–1
	Approved (AP)	0·4	0·2	0·3	0·3	0–3	0–2	0–3
	Acknowledged (AC)	0·6	0·4	0·8	0·6	0–2	0–3	0–5
	Not Evaluated (NE)	0·1	0·1	0·2	0·2	0–2	0–1	0–2
	Neutrally Rejected (NR)	0·2	0·4	0·1	0·2	0–2	0–5	0–1
	Critically Rejected (CR)	0·0	0·1	0·0	0·0	0	0–1	0
ELABORATING	Supported (SP)	0·0	0·1	0·0	0·0	0–1	0–1	0
	Approved (AP)	0·2	0·1	0·3	0·2	0–3	0–1	0–3
	Acknowledged (AC)	0·3	0·7	0·3	0·4	0–2	0–3	0–4
	Not Evaluated (NE)	0·1	0·1	0·1	0·1	0–3	0–1	0–1
	Neutrally Rejected (NR)	0·0	0·1	0·0	0·1	0–1	0–1	0
	Critically Rejected (CR)	0·0	0·0	0·0	0·0	0	0	0
CONVERGENT	Supported (SP)	0·6	0·2	0·3	0·4	0–6	0–2	0–3
	Approved (AP)	1·8	1·6	2·0	1·8	0–10	0–6	0–11
	Acknowledged (AC)	3·4	4·1	3·1	3·5	0–16	0–15	0–8
	Not Evaluated (NE)	0·3	0·6	0·2	0·4	0–2	0–3	0–2
	Neutrally Rejected (NR)	0·9	0·9	0·4	0·7	0–5	0–5	0–2
	Critically Rejected (CR)	0·1	0·1	0·1	0·1	0–1	0–2	0–2
PUPIL INITIATED	Supported (SP)	0·4	0·2	0·3	0·3	0–2	0–2	0–2
	Approved (AP)	0·8	0·7	0·8	0·8	0–3	0–3	0–4
	Acknowledged (AC)	0·8	1·1	1·1	1·0	0–4	0–5	0–6
	Not Evaluated (NE)	0·3	0·4	0·3	0·3	0–2	0–2	0–2
	Neutrally Rejected (NR)	0·4	0·2	0·2	0·3	0–2	0–3	0–1
	Critically Rejected (CR)	0·0	0·1	0·1	0·1	0	0–1	0–2

Tables 8 and 9 are each constructed from various combinations and weighting of the categories which we have described. Table 8 compares the incidence of various types of 'entry'—that is to say, teacher and pupil statements and questions to specify three scales. Table 9 compares various types of 'exit' (Teacher reaction) to specify three further scales.*

TABLE 8

Scales based on Contrasting Types of Entry.

Scale	Infants	Junior	Senior
Pupil Initiative	−0·6	−0·6	0·0
Cohesion	−3·9	−3·6	−3·4
Divergence	−5·9	−6·7	−4·6

* Stability coefficients for these scales are satisfactory: Medley, 1967.

TABLE 9

Scales based on Contrasting Types of Exit.

Scale	Infants	Junior	Senior
Feedback	−2·5	−4·1	−3·0
Valence	2·2	0·9	2·4
Enthusiasm	−2·9	−2·8	−2·6

We take Table 8 first. 'Pupil Initiative' is achieved by contrasting the number of interchanges beginning with a pupil question or statement (x) and those beginning with a teacher question or statement (y). Weighting is as follows: $x - \frac{1}{3}y$. In practice, this means taking from the average frequency of pupil initiated entries, one third of the sum of the average entries for Divergent, Elaborating and Convergent entries.

Entries in the Tables vary from negative values through zero to positive values. In each case, negative values indicates lack of the characteristic in question.

The scales are defined as follows (Medley, 1967) *Cohesion:* 'The teacher who scores high on Cohesion tends to ask interrelated questions; his discussions hang together more than do those of the average teacher'. *Divergence:* '... the teacher scoring high tends to prefer open-ended questions to closed, factual ones.' *Feedback:* 'Scores on this key will indicate how likely a teacher is to give his pupils feedback [information about the appropriateness of their response] about what they say about content'. *Valence:* 'Where Valence is high, pupils are more likely to be right than wrong when they talk about content'. *Enthusiasm:* 'The enthusiastic teacher praises a [pupil] for being right and also criticises him for being wrong more often than the average teacher does'.

CHAPTER X

The Theoretical Study: notes towards a Conceptual Framework for Education

Introduction

Since this is only one chapter in an already complex report, and because we want to keep the presentation of the Theoretical Study as simple and as short as possible, we have decided to omit much of the historical and experimental background to this part of the study.* This chapter in any case consists of little more than preliminary jottings based on classroom observation. In no sense should it be taken as a comprehensive statement of a theoretical position.

The Technological Study, described in Chapters I–VII, concerned those aspects of the teacher's task which might be undertaken by an auxiliary. In the Theoretical Study, we are concerned with those activities and interactions which comprise the teaching/learning situation.

Previous research in this area has usually been directed at the construction of instruments to measure classroom interaction. The technique employed has been to count the number of occasions on which certain kinds of fairly obvious behaviour (e.g., pupil-statements) occur and to compare the incidence of these events in different classrooms. OScAR 4V, described in the previous chapter, is one of the best-known examples of the technique. This approach has been remarkably successful in measuring those variables related to what might generally be called 'pupil-happiness'. However, as Medley and Mitzel (1963) point out, little or no success has been achieved in the use of such instruments to isolate variables which relate to pupil-learning and achievement.

We believe that a reason for the lack of success in this endeavour has been a failure to study systematically and in some depth what actually goes on in the classroom. As a result, what these instruments measure is relatively superficial.†

What we are suggesting is that it is necessary to preface the construction of an instrument such as OScAR 4V by a long process of clinical observation during which we examine actual classroom behaviour to see whether we can isolate those events which relate to pupil-learning. This is what we have tried to do in the Theoretical Study. It is too early yet to say whether the events we describe do relate to the degree and kind of pupil-learning. However, results so far look promising.

---

* For a review of the background, we refer the reader particularly to Gage (1963). Other useful sources are Bruner (1966), Taba (1962), Tibble (1966) and Biddle & Ellena (1964).

† A similar point is made by two writers in the field of general psychology, Holt (1950) and Donaldson (1963). They claim that *any* experimental study should be preceded by a period of preliminary observation during which hypotheses are formulated for subsequent testing.

We have already isolated aspects of the teaching/learning process which have been missed by conventional observational instruments. Classroom learning, for example, is clearly a *sequential* affair, and any system which ignores this is unlikely to isolate those variables related to pupil-learning. No teacher would teach by means of a series of unrelated statements or unrelated interchanges, yet this is all that classroom analysis has hitherto picked up. We have attempted, in the Theoretical Study, to develop a descriptive system which takes account of sequence.* It seems likely that if we can eventually develop an observational instrument from this system then we have some chance of measuring those variables which relate to pupil-learning.

The paradigms: the micro-paradigms

The work which we have done in the Theoretical Study, then, has been at the clinical level.† This does not mean, however, that our observation was undirected: we should soon have been overwhelmed by the complexity of the situation if this had been so. For reasons given above, we decided to try to isolate clinically those variables which are related to differential pupil-learning. This could have been done in a number of ways. We decided to do it by constructing paradigms or models of classroom behaviour, using as our initial building-blocks the following 'units' of behaviour:

Symbol	Unit
⇨	intended communication (verbal statement/question, or look or gesture)
◯	communication received *or* subject (pupil or teacher) clearly thinking
▢	subject observing a written communication *or* monitoring (e.g., teacher goes round class observing the quality of work)
▽	long-term memory *or* information store (e.g., books)
◎	subject engaged in an overt activity (as distinct from the covert activity of thinking)
▲	sequence interrupted and not resumed

These symbols, adapted from O & M usage, have the advantage that they are free of particular content—they are the same whatever is being

---

* It is true that OScAR 4V makes a step in this direction with the recording of complete interchanges between teacher and pupil (see page 57). It is probably necessary however to place these interchanges themselves in context: to make a 'map' of the lesson. The only other attempt of this kind which we have been able to trace is that of B. Othanel Smith (1959). In spite of a promising start, however, he tends to move away from a study of sequence to a comparative count of instances (albeit instances of a cognitive kind).

† 'Clinical' as distinct from 'experimental', at least in its formal sense. In clinical observation, no attempt is made at experimental design. From a few intensive clinical observations are developed hypotheses for subsequent testing at an experimental/statistical level.

communicated—and hence have the potential of demonstrating recurrent patterns of classroom behaviour. Two such patterns ('macro-paradigms') have in fact been isolated and will be described later (pages 65–71).

To produce a sequential record of classroom behaviour, our next task was to develop a method of relating and identifying these symbols. An example of the technique which we developed is given in Figure 6. On the left is the completed Record Form; on the right, the verbatim transcript from which the analysis was made.*

Reading from left to right across the sheet headings we have, first of all, a column for time. There follows a column for content used chiefly as a verbal prompt for the person doing the analysis to remind him of the content for the processes described in the paradigms. (For reasons given below, neither of these columns has been completed in the example given.) There follow five columns indicating the people whose behaviour is being recorded. The most economical way of indicating this, and one which has so far proved feasible, is a separate column for the teacher, two for individuals, and one each for group and class. Any individuals can be recorded in the 'Individual' columns. If it is necessary to distinguish among individuals within a sequence this can be indicated by numbers within the appropriate symbols in the columns. Different groups can be similarly distinguished if this is thought desirable.

Interactions amongst class members and with the teacher are thus conveniently grouped in one section of the chart.

The next group of columns provides information concerning the kind of behaviour being observed. These columns refer to teacher or pupils, the actual method of indicating which on any particular occasion being given below. In the column headed 'Experiencing' are entered items of behaviour such as 'playing with' sand or water, or with blocks or beads. Aesthetic experiences are also entered in this column. The next column is more straightforward and contains all instances of informational statements, where the primary concern is merely to convey information rather than to explain it. Thus the statement 'The capital of Scotland is Edinburgh' would be entered in this column. The column headed 'Structures' contains those verbal interchanges whose primary function is to explain rather than merely to convey information, for example where the teacher rephrases a question contained in a book so that the pupil can understand it more readily. The next two columns contain questions and answers (again from teacher or pupil). The Feedback columns are less easy to explain. Feedback is entered where the primary function of behaviour is to obtain or to provide knowledge of results. The positive column is used where the knowledge given or received indicates that the course of action was appropriate: inappropriate in the case of the negative column. Where feedback is merely sought, the 'Neutral' column is used. If the feedback is from pupil to teacher (P/T) then the teacher is obtaining information about the 'adequacy' of her teaching. (Thus if few or none of the pupils understand a new point she has made, as indicated by their wrong responses, then these responses give her information

---

* The analysis cannot be made during observation because of the speed with which the events occur: for the moment we have to carry out the analysis from a verbatim transcript or a videotape. To obtain a verbatim record of a lesson it is necessary to use experienced observers (preferably with tape recorders or employing shorthand)—but see page 71.

that she will probably have to restructure.) Where the feedback is in the opposite direction then the teacher (or material) is giving the pupil(s) information about the adequacy of their response or activity. In the columns 'Extrinsic Motivation, positive and negative', are entered examples of praise or punishment (clearly normally in the direction teacher/pupil).

The column headed 'procedural' contains two kinds of classroom behaviour. The first can be carried out only by the teacher or by her pupils; e.g., 'Open your books at page 10' or 'We would like to use the maths materials'. The second kind relates directly to the Technological Study and has to do with procedural items of a housekeeping nature. Where these occur they are labelled 'H/K'.

Entries can be made in more than one of these columns, where for example we have a Procedural Question; or Feedback combined with Extrinsic Motivation (e.g., 'Quite right'. 'Well done!').

The final columns, under the heading 'Media' are self-explanatory: book, blackboard, material (e.g., work cards), other: films, television, etc.

The symbols described on page 63 are entered in the columns for Teacher or for Pupil, thus indicating who is doing what. Further definition of the behaviour is provided by the 'Form of Activity or Communication' columns. The initial plan was merely to enter tally marks in these columns, linked to the 'people' entries by a horizontal line. On further consideration, however, it was decided to enter a 'T' (for teacher) or 'P' (pupil) or 'M' (material), etc., in these columns so that if totals of, say, pupil questions were required—as distinct from teacher questions—then these could be obtained without constant reference to the 'people' columns. (For 'horizontal' analysis—as distinct from vertical totalling—these letters are of course tautological.)

Entries in the media columns are indicated chiefly by ▽ unless the book, etc., asks a specific question of the pupil in which case arrows are used. The use of similar symbols for teacher, books, programmed learning, films, etc., should thus help point up the similarities and differences under these various conditions of learning.

The beginning of a sequence is indicated by any hatched symbol in the left-hand column: e.g., ◨

In the example given in Figure 6, the time-scale has been ignored.* For ease of cross-reference, items and analyses have been given numbers. The breakdown of the items and description of content provided at the right-hand side of Figure 6 are given only for the purpose of explanation. (In practice, a note in the 'content' column is sufficient.)

Another short example shows how the 'media' columns are used (see Figure 7).

The macro-paradigms

We refer to the individual symbols (and their non-recurrent inter-relations) as 'micro-paradigms'. Out of this level of analysis have come two recurrent patterns of interaction which we have called 'macro-paradigms'. These patterns were isolated during clinical analysis of our classroom observations.

* We are experimenting with appropriate time-scales for the accommodation of detailed educational interchanges. The present system is to provide a foolscap sheet for each ten-minute observational period. The number of interchanges which take place in some lessons, however, make it difficult to keep to this time-scale and it may be necessary to adopt a 5-minute scale.

FIGURE 6

Time	Content	Teacher	Individual	Individual	Group	Class	Form of activity or communication											Media			
							Experiencing	Informational statements	Structures	Question	Answer	Feedback			Extrinsic Motivation		Procedural	Book	Blackboard	Materials	Other
												Positive	Neutral	Negative	Positive	Negative					
1						○					T										
2						◎											P				
3		○									T.										
4	○					○					P										
5	Ditto 1–4																				
6		○				○					T										
	○					○					P										
	○					○					T/P———T/P										
7						○					T										
8						○									T/P						
9						○					T										
10		○															T				
11	◎																P H/K				
12	Ditto 10–11																				
13	◎										P/T										
14	Ditto 13																				
15	○										T/P etc										

66

Figure 6

1. Teacher: What animal did you like when you visited the zoo? (Question asked by teacher of class. The hatching indicating the beginning of a sequence.)

2. Class put up their hands (double circle for overt activity—classified as procedural).

3. Teacher selects individual pupil to give response (again procedural, this time by teacher).

4. Pupil gives reply 'Snake' which is heard by teacher and class. (The double-headed arrow indicates that both teacher and class were addressed.)

5. In the actual lesson this question and answer pattern was repeated several times. In practice this can be indicated by a bracket with ditto marks covering the appropriate time-scale. (It is extremely likely that such a pattern would be one of the macro-paradigms indicated below.)

6. Some of the pupils shouted out their answer before the teacher selected them for reply. The paradigm analysis indicates in the last line of this section that the teacher accepted the reply (+ve feedback) but asked the pupils not to shout out in future (negative extrinsic motivation).

7. After extensive questioning and answering of this kind the teacher listed all the animals which the pupils had mentioned. 'That's a snake we've had, and a crocodile and a lizard and a polar bear, etc.' This is clearly a kind of structuring of the lesson (summarising for what is to follow).

8. First, however, she gives general praise 'You have done well'.

9. The teacher then explains that the pupils are going to make a frieze of the zoo, each painting his favourite animal.

10. She then nominates individual pupils to give out paint and brushes.

11. & 12. Ditto.

13. Later she goes round the class observing the children's activities.

14. Ditto.

15. She tells a pupil that his animal will be too small to be seen, etc.

FIGURE 7

Time	Content	Teacher	Individual	Individual	Group	Class	Form of activity or communication											Media			
							Experiencing	Informational statements	Structures	Question	Answer	Feedback			Extrinsic motivation		Procedural	Book	Blackboard	Materials	Other
												Positive	Neutral	Negative	Positive	Negative					

Structuring and Media

10.12 Now then, close your books. Remember we were talking about DECIMALS yesterday. What does decimal mean? (No answer given or sought.) 'December'. 'Decade'. It comes from the Latin '*decem*'. It means counting in tens.

10.13 (Teacher demonstrates on blackboard). The one whole item becomes tens and units:

	T	U
	1	1
	2	2
	3	3
	4	4
10.14	5	5
	6	6
	7	7
	8	8
	9	9
	1	0

10.15 (Teacher demonstrates with squared graph paper.) This is how one is broken into 10ths, 1/10th, 2/10ths, etc. It's only a *bit* after the point. Instead of writing $1\frac{1}{10}$th, I write 1 (whole one) and $\frac{1}{10}$th or ·1, i.e., 1·1.

At the level of macro-paradigms, we are seeking not only a description of overt events but also a description of those covert events which must be going on to account for learning. In this way, we hope eventually to link an analysis of classroom observation with what is known about the psychology of human learning.

For this purpose, it is necessary to introduce the following additional symbols:

      ⊓   = short-term (temporary) memory

      D   = delay

The basic pattern for the *instructional* macro-paradigm is as follows: (we use only the teacher and pupil columns from the analysis sheet for illustration purposes):

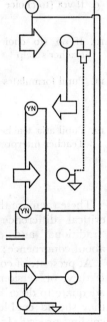

Teacher   Pupil

1. Teacher structures information or question

2. Teacher communicates to pupil
   Pupil processes information/question and stores (temporarily)

3. Pupil communicates interpretation to teacher/answers question
   Teacher compares response with expected response and checks whether the two are congruent

4. If yes, teacher gives positive feedback to pupil (who stores permanently) plus, perhaps a positive sanction

5. Teacher asks, 'Is lesson over?'
   If yes, ends lesson. If no, returns to beginning of paradigm with new question/statement

6. If no (to choice at stage 3) teacher gives negative feedback (and perhaps negative sanction)

7. Teacher decides to: ask questions again, restructure, or apply 'stop rule' (gives up for the moment and stores this information)

It will be seen that the instructional paradigm is a more detailed illustration of the interchanges which are described in Figure 6. Thus items 1 and 4 in Figure 6 together constitute the overt aspects of an instructional interchange. Items 2 and 3 are procedural and in this sense non-essential. Feedback to the pupils (and sanctions) fail to occur overtly (it is usually taken by the pupils that silence means affirmation, unless accompanied by a frown).

We turn now to the typical *self-instructional* paradigm. This model is typical of activity methods. Again we attempt to describe as far as possible the covert as well as the observable aspects of the process.

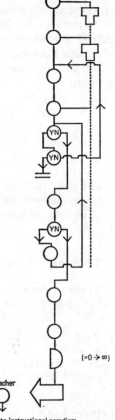

1. Pupil decides to undertake project/selects activity, etc.

2. Pupil plans project, activity, etc.

3. Pupil starts (continues) project

4. Pupil checks progress against plan

5. Pupil decides whether they are sufficiently congruent

6. If yes, pupil decides whether plan is complete

7. If no (to choice at stage 5) pupil attempts to decide what he did wrong

8. Pupil asks whether solution is available

9. If yes (to choice at stage 8) pupil modifies result

10. If no (to choice at stage 8) pupil decides to ask teacher's help

11. Pupil formulates question

12. Pupil asks teacher for help ⎫
    Teacher interprets   ⎬

To loop into instructional paradigm

These then are the macro-paradigms. As they stand, they define one of the critical differences—perhaps *the* critical difference—between so-called 'traditional' and 'progressive' education as being who makes the decision about congruence: pupil or teacher.

At present, of course, the macro-paradigms have the status of hypotheses. If they, or versions of them, are validated—that is to say, if they prove adequate to describe the various interchanges which occur in our records— they should enable us to achieve a considerable simplification in the re- cording process. Instead of having to record each item of behaviour separ- ately, it would then be possible to record recurring patterns by code letter and to concentrate instead on unusual occurrences.

In each of these macro-paradigms it goes without saying that not all of the behaviour described need be conscious. All that we claim here (as in computer-simulation of human behaviour) is that the teacher and pupils act *as if* they had made certain decisions. Teachers, for example, will not always ask themselves whether the lesson is over, but to carry on with the lesson as they do, they act as if such a question had been asked.

Returning to the actual examples taken from classroom observation, examination of Figure 6 will show that the paradigms can give an interesting view of the whole lesson if examined column by column. A comparison of the number of hatched arrows (initiated interchanges) in the teacher and Individual/Group/Class columns for example indicates the balance between teacher and pupil contribution to the lesson. More generally, and as a result of their analytical nature, the paradigms should make it easier to understand the extremely complex set of processes which comprise the classroom situation. The simplification yielded by our paradigms is at least two-fold: it reduces what would otherwise be a verbal record to symbolic terms: and it describes events in terms of 'process' rather than 'context'. The context consists of the teacher, the classroom, blackboard, materials, etc. What the paradigms attempt is to emphasise what these *do*—in relation, of course, to what the children do—that is to say, the paradigms throw into relief the processes which normally take place in the classroom context. This emphasis on process—and on the sort of formal representation implied above —should enable us systematically to resynthesise the classroom in different forms: that is to say, should enable us to suggest *other* possible contexts for these educational processes. This could have important implications not only for the role of the auxiliary but also for the place in the classroom of such developments as audio-visual materials, team teaching and programmed learning and also for the function of the teacher. In the case of the teacher's function, the paradigms should help isolate what can be done only by the teacher because of her special skills.

The symbols used in the paradigms assume a particular theoretical position and this is perhaps inevitable. (The process of model-building, and indeed of theory-construction, can be seen as the *imposing* of a structure on one's observations. Models—and theories—are not correct or wrong; they are more, or less, appropriate.) These paradigms presuppose that, where pupils learn at all (other than by a process of conditioning) they are to some extent active and 'self-organising'. This is not to say that they are necessarily physically active, nor that their activity can be observed, but that thinking is an active process. The teacher is not faced with the passive organisms of classical behaviourist psychology but with pupils who have aims of their own, who sift, judge and relate what the teacher says to their own past experience,* however they are treated by the teacher. Of course it is possible (and economical of effort) to treat pupils as if they were inert, and under appropriate conditions (e.g., the threat of a test) pupils will organise themselves to learn in this way. However, 'Primary Education in Scotland' (1965) and its predecessor, 'The Primary School in Scotland' (1950) both mark a move away from this conception of the pupil. There are grounds for hope that psychological and educational conceptions of the child are once again converging.

Towards a conceptual framework for education

The paradigms have been presented thus far as a means of describing and isolating certain forms of classroom behaviour prior to the construction of an

---

* Readers may recognise in this description a reflection of the recent revolution in psychological thinking, pioneered by Hebb in 1949 (although the seeds were there even in Watson's own writing: see, for example, 'Psychology from the Standpoint of a Behaviorist', 1924), and demonstrated especially in the work of Harlow (1949), Festinger (1957), Hunt (1961), Miller, Galanter and Pribram (1959), and Piaget (passim).

instrument for the measurement of classroom interaction. They could also have other and perhaps more important uses. In teacher-training, for example, they might be employed as a means of defining certain teaching-skills; and in the development of a conceptual framework for education the paradigms might be used as a means of specifying the *implementation* stage of the educational process. It is to this latter use of the paradigms that we now turn.

The term 'conceptual framework' is used here to mean an early stage in the construction of a theory of education. A conceptual framework differs from a theory in that it cannot be tested in the traditional way. That is to say, specific deductions cannot be made from it which, if true, will verify the theory and which, if false, will disprove it—the view of science propounded by Popper (1959). A conceptual framework cannot be tested in this way because it is not sufficiently precise and unambiguous. (Conceptual frameworks, however, may eventually develop into theories.) The conceptual framework, however, can be tested in a less stringent way, and it is this: we should, by classroom observation, and perhaps from a study of the literature, attempt to find behaviour which cannot be reliably classified according to the system. The system can then be modified to encompass the observed behaviour, either in terms of additions or modifications to the system. This approach is closer to the view of science put forward by Sparkes (1962), one of Popper's critics, and it is the one we have adopted here.

The conceptual framework which we describe here has three levels—those of aims, implementation and outcome. As we have said, the level of implementation has been described in terms of the paradigms. Outcome we see for the moment as a mirror-image of aims and, although the area of educational outcome presents its own problems, notably evaluation, the two areas are certainly closely related. (Specify aims operationally and one has gone a long way towards solving the problems of evaluation of outcome.)

We have attempted to describe the level of aims in terms of Bloom's 'Taxonomy of Educational Objectives', the best and most systematic analysis available. Our attempt has led to several modifications in Bloom's system and we shall concentrate on the areas which require modification if his system is to provide an adequate description.

Bloom distinguishes three 'domains' of aims: the Cognitive domain, the Affective domain and the domain of Motor Skills. The Cognitive domain corresponds roughly to the area of thinking, and the Affective domain to feeling and moral behaviour.

Bloom subdivides the Cognitive domain into Knowledge on the one hand and Intellectual Abilities and (Intellectual) Skills on the other. Knowledge is itself subdivided into Knowledge of Specifics (e.g.,facts); Knowledge of ways and means of dealing with Specifics (e.g., conventions); and Knowledge of Universals and Abstractions (e.g., theories). The categories which comprise Intellectual Abilities and Skills range from Comprehension (e.g., ability to extrapolate) to Evaluation (judgements in terms of internal evidence and in terms of external criteria).

The Affective domain is organised as a hierarchy, ranging from Attending, through Responding, Valuing (including commitment), Organisation (e.g., of a value system) to what Bloom calls 'Characterisation by a Value or Value Complex' (e.g., 'confidence in his ability to succeed' and 'develops a consistent philosophy of life'). The principle which underlies this classification is that of 'internalisation'. Put rather crudely, externally applied sanctions (rewards and punishments) are gradually internalised in the course of the child's development so that he becomes interested in what has been rewarded in the past (and conversely with punishment). These interests gradually become organised into a value system and eventually into a philosophy of life.

A classification is not provided for the Third Domain. As Bloom says '. . . we find so little done about [motor skills] in secondary schools or colleges that we do not believe the development of a classification of these objectives would be very useful at present.' (Pages 7–8, Vol. 1.)

Clearly it is impossible to do justice to the two volumes of the Taxonomy in the space of a few pages and anyone who wished to develop the conceptual framework as we envisage it would have to consult the original volumes. Enough may have been said, however, to help clarify the general meaning of the three domains if not to show how to use them.

Bloom's system was devised by a committee of college and university examiners and it is therefore perhaps hardly surprising that it should require modification when applied to primary education. Modifications in this direction, however, provided that they do not affect the applicability of the system in other areas, should help to make the system more general and are to be welcomed.

Observation in class and discussion with teachers suggest that the first modification should be in terms of the addition of a developmental dimension to the Taxonomy. The Taxonomy tends to concentrate on the end-product of learning and omits any systematic consideration of concept *formation*. Put in the context of Piaget's theory of the development of thinking (see e.g., 1950) the Taxonomy should be extended to provide a description of aims related to the pre-operational, the concrete and the formal operational stages of thinking.

Since Bloom's system is conceived chiefly in terms of higher education we suggest for the analysis of the aims of Primary School teachers an additional domain, that of the basic educational skills—the old 3Rs. This is not strictly a 'domain' since each of the basic educational skills overlaps the other domains —e.g., Reading has a motor skill component as well as a cognitive component. Although not all teachers would teach these skills formally, all would agree that their attainment is basic to Primary Education and hence, for want of a better solution, it seems necessary to include them as a separate domain at this stage.

Again Bloom's system appears to relate chiefly to aims as conceived by the teacher for the pupils: although the most important aspect of the problem this is by no means the whole story. Pupils, as well as teachers, have aims and it might be predicted that unless teachers' and pupils' aims coincide classroom education will remain less effective that it would otherwise be.* The picture is even more complicated than this: teachers have aims with reference to their pupils and these may be long-term (e.g., helping them achieve an understanding of number) or short-term (e.g., learning a particular number

---

* This argument may seem to have totalitarian overtones. It need not have. At the lowest level, if pupils' aims are (and they often appear so in boys at the junior stage!) to avoid learning at all costs then clearly they are going to learn less than they otherwise might. At a higher level, an identity of aims does not necessarily imply that pupils take over these aims uncritically.

combination or completing a painting which they have spontaneously undertaken). Teachers also have long-term aims for themselves (e.g., promotion) and short-term aims for themselves (e.g., enjoying their teaching on a particular day). Similarly pupils have long-term aims and short-term aims with reference both to themselves and to the teacher. All of these aims may be in the Cognitive domain, the Affective domain, or Motor-skill domain.

Potential conflict or agreement between the aims of teacher and pupils can be specified in a 32-cell matrix: (we ignore for the moment the Motor-skill domain):

TABLE 10

Aims of Teacher

		with reference to pupils		with reference to teacher	
		short-term	long-term	short-term	long-term
with reference to pupils	short-term	cognitive 1 affective	cognitive 2 affective	cognitive 3 affective	cognitive 4 affective
	long-term	cognitive 5 affective	cognitive 6 affective	cognitive 7 affective	cognitive 8 affective
with reference to teacher	short-term	cognitive 9 affective	cognitive 10 affective	cognitive 11 affective	cognitive 12 affective
	long-term	cognitive 13 affective	cognitive 14 affective	cognitive 15 affective	cognitive 16 affective

(left margin label: **Aims of Pupils**)

Cell 1 specifies potential conflict or agreement between the short-term aims of the pupils for themselves and the short-term aims of the teacher for the pupils; i.e., do the short-term aims of the pupils for themselves conflict with the short-term aims of the teacher for the pupils? Similarly cell 12 specifies potential conflict or agreement between the short-term aims of the pupils for the teacher and the long-term aims of the teacher for herself. Clearly some cells are more important than others—e.g., cell 2 is more important than, say, cell 15. But all are possible.

74

Two questions arise: is this model relevant to the description of classroom variables? And can we measure the variables sufficiently precisely to enable us to use the model? Both questions are empirical ones and can only be answered by trying out the model. (Since the need for some such description was seen as a result of classroom observation, it seems as if the answer to the first question will be 'yes' or at least 'partly').*

Before concluding this section, it might be worth making a few general observations about aims, some of them obvious, others perhaps less obvious.

(a) A teacher's aims are seldom confined to one domain. One hopes that as mathematics is taught (primary aim, cognitive) so a life-long interest in the subject will develop in at least some of the pupils (secondary aim, affective). Some subjects, e.g., art, are taught with affective aims to the fore. Cogntiive aims (e.g., knowledge of the laws of perspective) are here secondary. There is a conflict although perhaps not at an official level about which aims are appropriate for religious education: whether affective aims should be uppermost (i.e., commitment) or whether cognitive aims are more appropriate at day school.

(b) What can be achieved depends in part of course on the age and maturity of the pupils concerned. It is unlikely that a primary school teacher would be concerned with developing a philosophy of life in her pupils. On the other hand, in introducing a completely new subject to a mature student, it is necessary to return to the concrete level.

(c) The emphasis on affective aims which characterised education in the United States until recently is being gradually replaced (see e.g., Bruner's work) by a cognitive emphasis. They presumably believe that they have tried the affective area and found it wanting. I believe that this rests on a misconception. Their attempts at affective education were restricted almost entirely to the fostering (and measuring) of 'class atmosphere'. There is a great deal to do in the affective area in terms of motivation. For example, cognitive dissonance (e.g., Festinger (1957)) as a means of achieving interest should be more frequently considered as an alternative to or as well as the more usual extrinsic reward.

(d) Again it might be added that teachers' aims are not necessarily conscious, far less expressed. One could test whether an articulated awareness of one's aims distinguished effective from ineffective teachers. It is certainly unlikely that awareness of one's aims would hinder effective teaching (except perhaps in the first stages of awareness) and it might be argued that the Education Departments and Colleges of Education should be doing more in this direction.

Summary of Chapter X

In this chapter we have described those aspects of the Survey which concerned the process of teaching and learning in the primary school. We first of all described paradigms or models for classroom behaviour; two macro-paradigms, recurrent patterns of behaviour, were specified—the Instructional and the Self-instructional.

---

* A recent study by Thelen (1967) examines the problem of matching teachers and pupils in teachable groups, although not in the terms which we have defined above.

An attempt was made to develop a conceptual framework for education, employing three levels—aims, implementation and outcome. Aims were specified in terms of Bloom's 'Taxonomy of Educational Objectives' with some additions based on primary school requirements and on considerations of matching teachers' and pupils' aims. The implementation level was specified in terms of the paradigms; and outcome was taken to be the mirror-image of aims.

GLOSSARY OF TERMS USED IN THE REPORT

Block: The term used in the study to indicate the method of deciding whether there are sufficient opportunities for Supervision to merit the presence of an auxiliary in a lesson. A full description of the technique is given in Appendix 'A' under the heading 'Supervision Blocks—Assessment of'.

Clinical method: The informal study of particular cases with the aim of generating hypotheses for subsequent clinical test. (One of the criticisms of current research techniques in the social sciences is that hypotheses tend to be thought up without first looking to see 'what actually happens'. It would appear that the chief criterion in research is often the elegance of the experimental design rather than the significance of the hypothesis. See, e.g., Taylor's 'Experimental Design: a Cloak for Intellectual Sterility', 1958.)

Conceptual framework: An early stage in theory construction (for further definition see page 72).

Instruction, Theory of: A theory which describes the cognitive aspects of the teaching/learning process.

Paradigm: A model, in symbolic terms, of an (educational) process (see pages 63–65 for further definition and examples).

Structure: A communication, usually verbal, whose primary function is to explain rather than merely to convey information; for example, where the teacher rephrases a question or statement contained in a book so that the pupil can understand it more readily.

Technological study: That part of the study which was devoted to the provision of information to enable headmasters and teachers to use auxiliaries as effectively as possible.

Theoretical study: That part of the study which was devoted to the analysis of the teaching/learning process.

Wave approach: An approach employing a technique of solution by successive refinement. (Since the problem which we were tackling required the construction of new analytical tools, we approached the problem by a series of 'Waves' during which these tools were forged. We tackled the main investigation only when we were satisfied that we could answer the questions we had asked ourselves. See also definition on page 3.)

REFERENCES

The references listed are to those books and journal articles actually mentioned in the Report. In the course of the two years we consulted and read many other sources which, although not mentioned directly, affected the course of the study.

Advisory Council on Education in Scotland (1950): 'The Primary School in Scotland'. Edinburgh; H.M.S.O.

Advisory Council on Education in Scotland (1965): 'Primary Education in Scotland'. Edinburgh; H.M.S.O.

Beck, S. J., and Molish, H. B. (eds.) (1959): 'Reflexes to Intelligence'. Illinois: Free Press.

Biddle, B. J., and Ellena, W. J. (eds.) (1964): 'Contemporary Research on Teacher Effectiveness'. New York: Holt, Rinehart and Winston.

Bloom, B. J. et al (1956 and 1964): 'Taxonomy of Educational Objectives'. Handbooks I and II. London: Longmans, Green.

Bruner, J. S. (1966): 'Toward a Theory of Instruction'. Cambridge, Massachusetts: Harvard University Press.

Central Advisory Council for Education (England) (1967): 'Children and their Primary Schools'. (2 vols.). London: H.M.S.O.

Donaldson, M. C. (1963): 'A Study of Children's Thinking'. London: Tavistock Publications.

English, H. B. and English, A. C. (1958): 'A Comprehensive Dictionary of Psychological and Psychoanalytical Terms'. London: Longmans, Green.

Festinger, L. (1957): 'A Theory of Cognitive Dissonance'. Evanston, Illinois: Row, Peterson.

Gage, N. L. (ed.) (1963): 'Handbook of Research on Teaching'. Chicago: Rand, McNally.

Harlow, H. F. (1949): 'The Formation of Learning Sets'. Psychological Review, 56, 51–65.

Hebb, D. O. (1949): 'The Organisation of Behavior'. New York: Wiley.

Holt, R. R. (1950): 'Some Statistical Problems in Clinical Research'. Educ. and Psychol. Measurement, 10, 609–627; reprinted in Beck, S. J. and Molish, H. B., 1959, pp. 512–519 (q.v.).

Hunt, J. McV. (1961): 'Intelligence and Experience'. New York: Ronald Press.

Medley, D. M. (1967): Personal communication.

Medley, D. M., Impelletteri, J. T., and Smith, L. H. (1966): 'Coding Teacher Behaviors in the Classroom: A Manual for Users of OScAR 4V'. New York: Division of Teacher Education of the City University of New York.

Medley, D. M., and Mitzel, H. E. (1963): 'Measuring Classroom Behavior by Systematic Observation. In Gage, N. L. pp. 247–328 (q.v.).

Miller, G. A., Galanter, E. H., and Pribram, K. H. (1959): 'Plans and the Structure of Behavior'. New York: Holt.

Park, C. et al (1956): 'Bay City Michigan Experiment'. Journal of Teacher Education, June, 1956.

Piaget, J. (1950): 'The Psychology of Intelligence'. London: Routledge and Kegan Paul.

Plowden Report: see Central Advisory Council for Education.

Popper, K. R. (1959): 'The Logic of Scientific Discovery'. London: Hutchinson.

Smith, B. Othanel (1959): 'A Study of the Logic of Teaching'. Co-operative Research Project No. 258 U.S. Dept. of Health, Education and Welfare, Washington, D.C. (Available from ERIC Document Reproduction Service ED 000–895).

Sparkes, J. J. (1962): 'Scientific Method'. Bull. Inst. of Physics and the Physical Soc., 13, November, 1962, No. 11.

Taba, H. (1962): *'Curriculum Development: Theory and Practice'*. New York: Harcourt, Brace and World.

Taylor, J. G. (1958): *'Experimental Design: a Cloak for Intellectual Sterility'*. B. J. Psychol., *49*, 106–116.

Thelen, H. A. (1967): *'Classroom Grouping for Teachability'*. New York: Wiley.

Tibble, J. W. (ed.) (1966): *'The Study of Education'*. London: Routledge and Kegan Paul.

Watson, J. B. (1924): *'Psychology from the Standpoint of a Behaviorist'*. Philadelphia: Lippincott.

Yale–Fairfield Study of Elementary Teaching (1959): *'Teacher Assistants'*. New Haven, Connecticut.

ACKNOWLEDGEMENTS

I should like to acknowledge the help and guidance of the Consultative Committee, its Chairman, Dr. George Reith, and the Scottish Education Department Representative, Mr. John McClellan, in the planning and execution of the Survey. Its members gave unstintingly of their time and knowledge both formally, at the meetings which punctuated the progress of the Survey, and informally by letter, telephone conversation and private meeting. Especial mention should be made of the contribution of Mr. N. M. Keegan, Secretary to the Consultative Committee. The appearance of this Report in print is in great part due to his untiring efforts.

Callander Park College of Education provided a hospitable environment for the intensive work which our two years of commitment to the Survey required. We are most grateful to Mrs. Leggat, the Principal, and to the members of her staff, academic and clerical.

I should also like to acknowledge the help of the following persons and institutes: Dr. A. Pilliner of the Godfrey Thomson Unit for Educational Research, Mr. W. Fearnley of the Scottish Education Department, and Messrs. G. Horrobin, D. Ohlman and W. Bytheway, of the Medical Sociology Research Unit, all of whom provided us with statistical advice for the various aspects of the Survey; Mr. Norman Lawrie and members of the Department of Operational Research at Strathclyde University for advice on the technological analysis; and the Directors of Education, members of Her Majesty's Inspectorate and Primary School Advisers who facilitated our school visits.

As a Team we of course owe a special debt of gratitude to the teachers and head teachers of the many schools we visited. Without their help and co-operation the Survey would have been quite impossible; without the welcome which they extended to us the Survey could not have been the pleasant experience it was for Team members. Thanks are similarly extended to the teachers, head teachers and administrative staff in Oxfordshire, Hertfordshire and Inner London who made our comparative visits to schools in those areas equally pleasant and rewarding.

I should like to thank Professor Donald Medley for his help and advice in the use and interpretation of his Observation Schedule and Record; and Dr. W. B. Inglis, former Principal of Moray House College of Education, for encouragement and advice.

Thanks are also extended to the Librarians of Callander Park, Moray House and Jordanhill Colleges of Education for their help and forbearance.

As Research Director and Team Leader I should like to express my warmest thanks and deepest gratitude to my Research Team: to Miss Ann B. MacDonald; Dr. Francine M. Taylor; Mr. Donald J. MacLennan and Mr. W. N. C. Wardrop. This has been in every sense a co-operative project and without their help, advice and friendship the Survey could never have been completed. As a Team our thanks are extended to Mrs. Ann Cowie, our Secretary, who has dealt efficiently with the manuscripts of the various drafts of the Report, has filed and retrieved the vast amounts of information which we have collected, and (with the occasional help of Mrs. Margaret

Munro) has generally ensured the smooth running of the clerical aspects of the Survey.

Finally, I should like to thank the following for permission to quote short extracts from their publications:

The American Educational Research Association   *'A Handbook of Research on Teaching'*, edited by N. L. Gage.

David McKay Company, Inc.   *'Taxonomy of Educational Objectives'*, Handbook I, edited by B. S. Bloom, Handbook II, by D. R. Krathwohl, B. S. Bloom and B. B. Masia.

'A Comprehensive Dictionary of Psychological and Psychoanalytical Terms', by H. B. English and A. C. English.

JOHN H. DUTHIE

Department of Education,
University of Stirling.
December, 1968.

Rule Book

Auxiliary in supervisory charge of part class

PROBLEM: teacher taking Physical Education in playground. Part class left in class-room on own volition, continuing with activities. Can we recommend auxiliary in classroom to supervise? Auxiliary can be justified in classroom (subject of course to the usual judgments concerning gainful and safe employment—see Supervision Check-list) on this basis on the grounds that teachers will do this only when they are able to provide sufficient structuring at the beginning of the lesson thus leaving the auxiliary in charge of only the supervision aspects.

Buffer, Auxiliary as

> Time as instances only, irrespective of how long child has to wait; similarly for pupil clearly unoccupied.

Category 'B' Duties (i.e., partly-fixed)

> Period should be defined (in notes column) during which duty must be done. (E.g., registration must be done between 9 a.m. when the children arrive and 10 a.m. which is the (presumed) legal limit.)

Equipment, Distribution of

> Asking for new jotter:
>
> B if teacher required pupils to anticipate requirements before lesson starts.
> D if pupil asks during lesson.

Housekeeping jobs done by Children/Housekeeping/Supervision borderline

PROBLEM: boy spills water; teacher tells boy to clear it up. Is this Supervision or Housekeeping?

> Judgment must be made on whether the pupil will benefit educationally from doing it himself. (The teacher would give the auxiliary preliminary guidance on this for class in question.) If so, the situation is classified as Supervision, if not, assume the auxiliary will do it and classify as Housekeeping. (Whether it is classified as Supervision or Housekeeping will probably depend on the age of pupil.)

Housekeeping and Supervision occurring together

> If the need for Supervision has been created simply because the teacher is doing Housekeeping then the auxiliary would do the Housekeeping and we do not record Supervision.
> If Supervision would be necessary even if teacher were not doing Housekeeping of this type, then we record both Supervision and Housekeeping and later reallocate the Housekeeping.
> Timing would not be total length of the Housekeeping duty, e.g., registration would have to be taken as average for classes of this kind where registration is uninterrupted.

Materials, Difficulties with

Where the difficulty is simply in the acquisition of material classify as House-keeping B or D (see: equipment, distribution of).

Where difficulty is in the *use* of material, classify as Supervision.

One-Teacher schools: Block system

Duties can be done using the classroom as a unit hence the block system is not required. Auxiliary would be on call for virtually all duties since in a one-teacher school, the classroom=the school=the unit.

In analysis, all that is required is the totalling of all duties and examination of their distribution.

Outside-classroom Activities: Supervision of

As for auxiliary in supervisory charge of part-class (q.v.).

Parallel Occurrence of Duties

Record duties in parallel and enter in notes column whether they can be
(i) reallocated (record 'end on')
or whether they must
(ii) occur simultaneously (record 'simul').

Playtime Supervision

Auxiliary can be justified in classroom subject to the usual judgments concerning gainful and safe employment (see: Supervision Check-list), on the grounds that she would not be involved in actual or potential structuring.

Pupil clearly unoccupied

It has been observed in some classrooms that pupils are for certain lengths of time clearly unoccupied. It is not possible for the Team to decide in every case whether this is the teacher's deliberate policy. It is, however, necessary to have a set of criteria to identify opportunities for auxiliary help in terms of periods during which pupils are apparently unoccupied. The criteria which were adopted are given below:

1. Maximum number of children apparently unoccupied at any one time: 3
2. Maximum length of time during which any one pupil should remain unoccupied:

Infants: 4 minutes
Junior: 3 minutes
Senior: 2 minutes

There are two recorded forms of lack of purposeful activity

1. Interruption (P. unoccupied)
2. P. unoccupied: P(otential)

In the case of interruptions, the teacher has felt it necessary to remark on the pupil's lack of purposeful activity. In the second case, the teacher has not remarked on the pupil's lack of purposeful activity but the period of inactivity has lasted for at least a minimum length (defined above). We are not stating that an auxiliary could deal with all such situations—simply that her presence might avoid the inactivity which we record.

N.B. Irrespective of length of inactivity, these duties are recorded as *instances*, not as periods.

Supervision Blocks: assessment of

PROBLEM: Since supervisory duties occur in short bursts it is impracticable to summon an auxiliary for individual instances of Supervision as they occur in the classroom. On the other hand, supervisory assistance, if provided, is required for the whole activity or lesson rather than for any particular part of it: i.e., the supervisory block should be justified (or otherwise) in terms of a whole lesson rather than particular parts of it. (Since in practice we have found it extremely difficult to predict—even with hindsight—what particular aspects of a lesson would have required auxiliary supervision, it appears unlikely that teachers could predict their own requirements in this respect.) What we are attempting here then is to define the basis on which auxiliaries would be made available for a whole lesson or activity: the 'block' referred to above.

1. In deciding whether to block in supervisory instances, we examine first the form of class-organisation. If it is non-class-teaching we define its time-limits (i.e., when it started and when it stopped). Next we examine for content within this period. If content changes for class as a whole, then we define the content time-limits and block for these. (If activities are running in parallel rather than end-on, and only the teacher changes from one content-group to another, this is recorded as a continuation of the same lesson as regards content.)

2. Once the potential location of the block has been defined as above, we must decide whether there are sufficient supervisory instances within the block to justify the presence of an auxiliary. Here there are two criteria and the presence of an auxiliary can be justified as one or other of these: *frequency:* teacher should be allowed ten-minute periods free from interruption as a minimum. Hence interruptions should not exceed one in ten minutes: *time:* the teacher should not require to spend more than one minute in three on average in supervisory duties over the block as a whole.

3. Note that where a gap of 15 minutes or more occurs in opportunity for supervisory duties, we assume that this would justify the departure of the auxiliary in practice and hence do not classify such a lesson as a block. Note also, however, that housekeeping usually runs in parallel and can be done by the auxiliary during pauses in supervisory duties.
The minimum length of lesson which would justify the supervisory presence of an auxiliary is put at 15 minutes.
Supervision blocks can be extended at either end if D and E Housekeeping Duties occur just prior to, or just after, a Supervision block.

Supervision Check-list

PROBLEM: In situations in which the teacher is actively teaching the class and all pupils are engaged upon identical activities, there is no scope for supervisory auxiliary assistance. Where pupils are working in groups or as individuals, however, auxiliary assistance may be required. The check-list given below has been drawn up in order that decisions can be made on the need for such assistance in particular cases.

A. Is teacher doing potential auxiliary Supervision Duties?

If yes, record (*from check-list below*)
If no, when the teacher is occupied with individual or group are others gainfully and safely employed? *If not, could auxiliary help?* (i.e., are children being held up for any of the reasons listed below?)

B. *Check-list* (referring to A and/or B)

    1. Teacher dealing with one of several groups during activity lesson.
    2. Objective marking required to enable pupils to proceed with lesson in hand.
    3. Are children following work cards in order?
    4. Are records of individual progress being kept?
    5. Children officially outside classroom unsupervised.
    6. Are children having problems with materials?
    7. Would teacher like pupils' drawings to be labelled?
    8. Could auxiliary act as 'buffer'? (I.e., 'intercepting' pupils who would otherwise interrupt teacher and deciding whether or not they require the teacher's help, otherwise dealing with it themselves—e.g., dealing with difficulties in the use of materials, complaints of one pupil against another, etc.)
    9. Read out test items.
   10. Help pupil find next assignment card.
   11. Children bring work for admiration.
   12. Encouragement of children working in groups while teacher works with individual pupil.

Note: Auxiliary must never be left in sole charge of whole class under actual or potential instruction.

See also: 'Supervision Blocks: Assessment of'
page 84 for further details.

Timing of Duties

Duties lasting for less than a half-minute are recorded as instances.
$\frac{1}{2}$ minute—less than $1\frac{1}{2}$ minutes recorded as one minute.
$1\frac{1}{2}$ minutes—less than $2\frac{1}{2}$ minutes recorded as two minutes, etc.
See: Housekeeping and Teaching Occurring Together.
See: Category 'B' Duties (i.e., partly-fixed).

APPENDIX B

Reliability Study of Timing and Classification of Duties

Prepared by Dr. A. E. G. Pilliner, Director, Godfrey Thomson Unit for Educational Research, Edinburgh.

I. Outline of experimental procedure

1. Two pairs of observers, F and A, and D and N, were concerned in this study. Each pair observed the duties called in this Survey A–E and Supervision. The pair F and A visited one set of classes, and the pair D and N another. The members of each pair independently estimated (1) the time taken for the performance of these duties; (2) the corresponding starting times; and (3) the nature of the duties thus timed.

II. Experimental results

2. The results of parts (1) and (2) above of this study are summarised in the following tables.

TABLES I. ESTIMATED TIMES TAKEN FOR DUTIES (IN MINUTES)

I(A). Observers F and A

$d = difference (F-A)$

Duty	A	B	C	D	E	Supervision		
Class	123	123	123	123	123	123	Total	
d			FREQUENCIES				f	Proportion
+2	001	000	000	000	000	—00	1	·008
+1	000	000	001	000	000	—00	1	·008
0	768	879	311	19 9 16	7 16 8	—31	129	·970
—1	000	000	000	1 0 0	0 0 0	—01	2	·015
	769	879	312	20 9 16	7 16 8	—32	133	1·001

I(B). Observers D and N

$d = difference (D-N)$

Duty	A	B	C	D	E	Supervision		
Class	123	123	123	123	123	123	Total	
d			FREQUENCIES				f	Proportion
+1	000	000	—01	000	—00	—00	1	·020
0	533	335	—13	233	—25	—00	41	·820
—1	010	100	—00	000	—00	—01	3	·060
—2	010	000	—00	000	—00	—20	3	·060
—3	000	000	—00	000	—00	—01	1	·020
—4	000	000	—00	000	—00	—10	1	·020
	553	435	—14	233	—25	—32	50	1·000

II(A). Observers F and A

$d = difference\ (F-A)$

Duty	A	B	C	D	E	Supervision		
Class	123	123	123	123	123	123	Total	
d				FREQUENCIES			f	Proportion
+1	000	000	000	303	000	−00	6	·045
0	467	674	312	15 9 7	5 15 7	−32	103	·780
−1	201	202	000	2 0 4	2 1 0	−00	16	·121
−2	000	001	000	0 0 2	0 0 1	−00	4	·030
−3	100	001	000	0 0 0	0 0 0	−00	2	·015
−4	000	000	000	0 0 0	0 0 0	−00	0	·000
−5	000	000	000	0 0 0	0 0 0	−00	0	·000
−6	000	000	000	0 0 0	0 0 0 ·	−00	0	·000
−7	001	000	000	0 0 0	0 0 0	−00	1	·008
	769	878	312	20 9 16	7 16 8	−32	132	·999

II(B). Observers D and N

$d = difference\ (D-N)$

Duty	A	B	C	D	E	Supervision		
Class	123	123	123	123	123	123	Total	
d				FREQUENCIES			f	Proportion
+2	000	000	−00	000	−00	−10	1	·019
+1	001	023	−00	100	−00	−10	8	·154
0	451	322	−12	101	−15	−11	30	·577
−1	101	110	−02	032	−10	−00	12	·231
−2	000	000	−00	000	−00	−01	1	·019
	553	455	−14	233	−25	−32	52	1·000

III. Discussion of the results in section II

3. The overall figures (see 'Total' columns, f and Proportion) suggest (i) that the F and A pair is more consistent than the D and N pair; and (ii) that within each pair, the consistency is high.

4. Thus Table 1(A) shows that F and A agree exactly in 97 per cent of their timings, and that in 99·3 per cent of them they do not differ by more than a minute either way. Table 1(B) shows that D and N agree exactly in 82 per cent, and in 90 per cent do not differ by more than a minute either way.

5. Similarly, Table II(A) shows that F and A agree in 78 per cent of their timings and that in 94·6 per cent of them they do not differ by more than a minute either way. Table II(B) shows that D and N agree in 57·7 per cent, and in 96·2 per cent do not differ by more than a minute either way.

6. This is a high degree of agreement—one of which a worker in behavioural sciences might well be envious. The extent to which the figures speak for themselves really obviates the necessity of expressing the agreement between observers by any

sort of statistical index. However, it may be of some interest to look more closely at the worst of the agreements, those recorded in Table I(B). The mean difference between the observers over the 50 observations is 0·30 minutes—that is, N appears to see a duty commencing that much earlier on the average than D does. The standard deviation of the differences is 0·85, so that the standard error of the main differences is 0·85/$\sqrt{50}$ or about 0·12. The observed mean difference (0·30) is about 2·5 times its standard error and is thus significant beyond the 5 per cent level. But how important is it practically?

7. Also, from the standard deviation of the difference (0·85) we can infer the standard error of a single observation made by either D or N. The estimate of this standard error is 0·85/$\sqrt{2}$=0·6 minutes approximately. This means that about 68 per cent of all observations, either by D or N will be in error by not more than 0·6 minutes either way. And if we take into account the fact that all observations are recorded to the nearest minute (so that, for example, an observation of 10 minutes means something over 9·5 minutes and under 10·5 minutes) we see that most of the standard error of 0·6 minutes is encompassed by the 'rounding error' arising from the practice of recording to the nearest minute.

8. As stated earlier, these computational reflections relate to the subgroup of observations in which the worst agreements are recorded. We can be fairly sure that the standard error of an observation is even smaller for the other subgroups in which the agreement is better.

IV. Consistency of observers:

9. (a) *From one class to another*

(b) *From one duty to another*

Two questions are asked:

(a) Disregarding the different nature of the duties, do the proportions of complete agreements vary from one class to another?

(b) Disregarding the different classes, do the proportions of complete agreements vary from one duty to another?

To answer question (a), we sum over duties to obtain class totals. To answer question (b) we sum over classes to obtain duty totals. The results and the derived proportions are tabulated below, together with the results of the statistical tests applied.

TABLE III

Time taken for duties—class to class variability
(duties combined)

Class		1	2	3	Total	
Observers F, A	No. of Agreements	44	42	43	129	
	No. of Observations	45	42	46	133	
	Proportions	0·978	1·000	0·935	0·970	x^2=0·101 (df 2) NS
Observers D, N	No. of Agreements	10	12	19	41	
	No. of Observations	11	17	22	50	
	Proportions	0·909	0·706	0·864	0·820	x^2=0·428 (df 2) NS

Table IV

Starting times for duties—class to class variability
(duties combined)

Class		1	2	3	Total	
Observers F, A	No. of Agreements	33	41	29	103	
	No. of Observations	45	42	45	132	
	Proportions	0·733	0·976	0·644	0·780	$x^2=3·258$ (df 2) NS
Observers D, N	No. of Agreements	8	10	12	30	
	No. of Observations	11	19	22	52	
	Proportions	0·727	0·526	0·545	0·577	$x^2=0·556$ (df 2) NS

Table V

Time taken for duties—duty to duty variability
(classes combined)

Duty		A	B	C	D	E	Supervision	Total	
Observers F, A	No. of Agreements	21	24	5	44	31	4	129	
	No. of Observations	22	24	6	45	31	5	133	
	Proportions	0·955	1·000	0·833	0·978	1·000	0·800	0·970	$x^2=0·37$ (df 5) NS
Observers D, N	No. of Agreements	11	11	4	8	7	0	41	
	No. of Observations	13	12	5	8	7	5	50	
	Proportions	0·846	0·917	0·800	1·000	0·583		0·820	$x^2=1·15$ (df 4) NS

Table VI

Starting times for duties—duty to duty variability
(classes combined)

Duty		A	B	C	D	E	Supervision	Total	
Observers F, A	No. of Agreements	17	17	6	31	27	5	103	
	No. of Observations	22	23	6	45	31	5	132	
	Proportions	0·773	0·739	1·000	0·689	0·871	1·000	0·780	$x^2=1·493$ (df 5) NS
Observers D, N	No. of Agreements	10	7	3	2	6	2	30	
	No. of Observations	13	14	5	8	7	5	52	
	Proportions	0·769	0·500	0·385		·667		0·577	$x^2=1·980$ (df 3) NS

V. **Discussion of the results in Section IV**

10. (a) *Is the proportion of complete observer agreements, whatever the duty, affected by the class in which the observations were made?*

The proportions in Tables III and IV answer this question. To illustrate: in Table III, Observers F and A, the expected proportion for each class is 0·970 (i.e., the mean proportion over all classes). The observed proportions are 0·978, 1·000 and 0·935 for classes 1, 2 and 3 respectively. The obtained value for x^2 indicates that the differences among these proportions are remarkably non-significant.

The other x^2's in Tables III and IV also indicate non-significant differences.

We conclude that the proportion of complete observer agreements is not affected by the class in which the observations were made.

11. (b) *Is the proportion of complete observer agreements, whatever the class, affected by the duty under observation?*

The proportions in Tables V and VI answer this question. In no case do they differ significantly for either pair of observers, from one duty to another.

We conclude that the proportion of complete observer agreement is not affected by the nature of the duty being observed.

VI. **Classification of duties**

12. The question here is: how well do the observers agree in their identification of the duties they observe?

For observers F and A, the data sheets report 'In agreement throughout'. The numbers of agreements for these two observers are 45 in the first class, 42 in the second, and 46 in the third.

We conclude that for observers F and A the agreement in classifying duties is eminently satisfactory.

For observers D and N, there is agreement in 11 out of 14 classifications on class 1; in 15 out of 19 on class 2; and there is complete agreement in 21 classifications on class 3. In all, there are 47 agreements out of 54 classifications, a proportion of almost exactly 87 per cent. The standard error of this percentage is 4·58 per cent. Regarding this set of 54 observations as a random sample from a population of such observations, we may assign confidence limits within which the population (parameter) may be presumed to lie. Since the distribution of mean proportions is increasingly skewed the further the proportion is from 50 per cent (except in very large samples), the standard procedure in estimating the confidence interval leads to inaccurate results. Instead, the Pearson–Hartley chart has been used. For a sample giving a mean of 87 per cent the 95 per cent confidence limits for the parameter value are approximately 72 per cent and 94 per cent. In short:

$$·72 < P < ·94 \quad \text{(95 per cent interval)}$$ where P is the parameter proportion.

This is a statistical statement. It is for those concerned in the study to decide whether the degree of agreement over classifications it represents is adequate for the purposes of the Survey.

VII. **Summary**

13. This study is concerned with the reliability of observations made on the timing and nature of duties carried out in schools.

14. The study shows that two pairs of observers all working independently agree substantially over the timings they allot (a) to the starting times for the duties, (b) to the periods of the duties. These levels of reliability have been shown to be adequate for statistical purposes.

15. The study shows that the observations made are equally consistent in different classes and for different duties.

16. The study indicates that one pair of observers is completely consistent in its classification of duties observed and that the other pair agrees in this respect in a substantial proportion of cases.

17. Subsequent informal checks have shown that agreement among all six possible combinations of observers is at a similar high level.

Statistical Report on Duty Timing

Prepared by Dr. A. E. G. Pilliner, Director, Godfrey Thomson Unit for Educational Research, Edinburgh

A. The pilot study (*Third wave*)

The general aim was to study the variability of the data emerging in the early stages of the Survey. Three cross-classifications were used. (i) 'Duties' were classified as A–E, Supervision and Preparation; (ii) 'School Size' as the number of teachers: 1, 2, 3–4, 5–6, 7–9, 10–13, and 14+; and (iii) 'Stage within Schools' as 1–2 (Infants), 3–4 (Junior), and 5–7 (Senior). The variate throughout was time in minutes. The main findings were as follows:

(1) There is no evidence that the overall time taken for the performance of duties A–E differs significantly from one category ('Infant', 'Junior' and 'Senior') to another.

(2) The times occupied by the individual duties A–E appear to differ significantly in most categories. Moreover, the *relative* times given to each of these duties are similar, whatever the category. The order, from the longest to the shortest time, is usually D, B, A, C, and E.

(3) Still considering the A–E duties, the replication mean standard error is about $11\frac{1}{2}$ minutes; that is, individual times for individual duties are very variable.

(4) The duties A–E (pooled), 'Supervision' and 'Preparation' occupy times in (or out of) the school day which are not significantly different if the categories 'Infant', 'Junior' and 'Senior' are considered overall.

(5) However, within these categories, 'Supervision' takes significantly longer in the 'Infant' category and significantly less time in the 'Senior' category.

It was pointed out at the end of the preliminary report to the Team that firm estimation of experimental error was an important requirement: 'The present study shows that the time taken for any one duty varies considerably from one occasion to another, even within one category and within one school size. This was only to be expected, and subsequent planning must be sufficiently flexible to take account of the inevitable variability. But for the planning to be efficient, a good estimate of this variability, in the form of replication error variance, is required.'

The report went on to make recommendations as to the design of further experiments in order to arrive at a more secure estimate of replication error variance than was possible in this earlier pilot study. These recommendations were incorporated in the design of the main study.

B. The main study (*Final wave*)

I. GENERAL OBJECTIVES

The general objectives were similar to those of the pilot study described above, namely: to obtain estimates of the times taken to perform the various duties at various levels in schools of various sizes (mean times), together with estimates of the variation to be expected in these times from one occasion to another (replication standard error). We should expect to set more store on the results of this main study than on those of its predecessor, (a) because experience gained in the pilot experiment should lead to a more appropriate experimental design; and (b) because in the course of the Survey it might have been found necessary to modify the nature and definition of some of the duties performed with consequent effects on the times taken for their performance. The information provided by this later study should therefore be more relevant than that of the earlier one to the situation that had developed by the end of the Survey.

To clear the ground further, it should be stated that because the results of the observer reliability study (Appendix B) were so satisfactory, no further work in this area was considered necessary.

II. THE DATA

(1) (i) The 'duties' we were asked to study were as follows:

A; B; C By Observation; C By Interview; Total C Duties; D; E; and S.

(ii) The 'school sizes' were designated:

1 class; 2 class; 3–4 class; 5–6 class; 7–9 class; 10–13 class; 14+ class.

(iii) The 'stages' within schools were designated:

I (Infant); J (Junior); S (Senior).

(2) Problems arose because the manner in which the data were classified on the data sheets we received could not be consistent from one 'school size' to another. In '1 class' schools (a sample of 7 schools), no distinction could be made between 'I', 'J' and 'S'. In '2 class' schools (a sample of 4), the trichotomy implied by 'I', 'J', 'S' was replaced by a somewhat blurred dichotomy. Thus in schools 1 and 3, the school classes* or grades were grouped as 1–3 and 4–7; in schools 2 and 4, the grouping was 1–4 and 5–7. In '3–4 class' schools (again 4), the category 'I' was always classes 1 and 2 in all 4 schools and the category 'J' always classes 3 and 4; the category 'S' consisted of classes 5–7 taken together in schools 1, 3 and 4, but in school 2 separate data for this category were presented for classes 5–6 and for class 7. Similar inconsistencies were apparent in the remaining 'school sizes'. While it had never been envisaged that we should throw all the different 'school sizes' into a single analysis, the inconsistencies exemplified above meant that no single analytical technique could be applied even *within* 'school sizes'. Instead, differences in treatment from one 'school size' to another became necessary. Details of these different treatments are presented in the following section.

III. STATISTICAL TREATMENT OF DATA

'1 Class' Schools

Table 1 shows the pattern of data for A duties. The pattern for all other duties was the same.

TABLE I

'1 Class' schools—data for A duties

School	1	2	3	4	5	6	7
IJS 1–7	14	5	2	4·5	7	18	61

(*Times in minutes*)

There is only one entry for each of the 7 schools comprising this sample, so that it is not possible to estimate within-school variability. It is conceivable that the time taken to perform a particular duty in a particular school is always much the same, though differing considerably from one school to another. If this were the case, it would be possible to state the mean time for a *particular* school and duty with that degree of precision warranted by the within-school variability as estimated from within-school replication for that duty.

---

* To avoid confusion, 'classes' or 'grades' refers here to the normal within-school organisation. This classification is to be distinguished from that used elsewhere in the study for 'school size' where the nomenclature was similar, i.e., 1 class, 2 class, etc.

93

However, our information is that within-school variability for a particular duty is considerable. This being so, there is not much point in attempting to obtain estimates for particular schools. Instead, we shall take it that these 7 schools are a random sample drawn from the population of schools. We shall then estimate the mean time to perform a particular duty as the mean of the 7 times observed in this sample of 7 schools, and the variability as the variance or standard deviation of these 7 times.

One minor point: all original times have been rounded off to the nearest minute for computational purposes.

Table II shows the mean times for the several duties and their standard deviations, as derived from the '1 class' sample of 7 schools.

TABLE II

'1 Class' schools. Duty time means and standard deviations

Duty	A	B	C by Obs.	C by Int.	Total C	D	E	S
Mean	16	9	11	64	75	14	4	135
s.d.	21	8	12	45	62	9	4	56

(*Times in minutes*)

It is apparent that there is considerable inter-school variability for each of these 8 duties. The standard deviation for A is indeed larger than the corresponding mean. The reason for this is the presence for school 7 of an observed time of 61 minutes, spectacularly different from the remaining 6 which range from 2 to 18 minutes (see Table I). On excluding this 'outlier', we find that the mean for the remaining 6 observations is between 8 and 9 minutes and their standard deviation 6 minutes. Whether such exclusion is justified is another matter. If we discount the possibility of an error in reporting, the occurrence of this observed time of 61 minutes is a fact. It was decided that on the whole it would be safer not to disregard such observations even though, as Table II shows, the standard deviations of times for many of the duties are disconcertingly high. These standard deviations are measures of the variability actually observed in the sample and its implications have to be accepted.

'2 Class' Schools

Table III shows the patterns of data for A duties. For all other duties the pattern was the same.

TABLE III

'2 Class' schools—data for A duties

School	1	3	School	2	4
Cl. 1–3	15	31·25	Cl. 1–4	16	21
Cl. 4–7	3·5	45	Cl. 5–7	4·25	3·75

(*Times in minutes*)

As stated earlier, the IJS trichotomy has been replaced by a dichotomy; for two of the schools, classes 1–3 and 4–7, and for the other two, classes 1–4 and 5–7. It was therefore decided for '2 class' schools to refer to 'Lower' and 'Higher' levels in which the 'Lower' level was either classes 1–3 or 1–4, and the 'Higher' level either classes 4–7 or 5–7.

The means and standard deviations computed for each 'level' and each 'duty' displayed considerable heterogeneity. For A duties, for example, while the difference

94

between the 'Lower' and 'Higher' level means (21 and 14 minutes) was not significantly different, that between the corresponding standard deviations (7 and 15 minutes) was significant. On the other hand, for duty C By Interview, the means differed significantly and the standard deviations did not. It was therefore decided that on the whole it would be safer to report means and standard deviations for each duty separately at each level. The results are shown in Table IV.

TABLE IV

'2 Class' schools. Duty time means and standard deviations

	Duty	A	B	C by Obs.	C by Int.	Total C	D	E	S
Lower Level	Mean	21	9	6	103	108	20	5	54
	s.d.	7	5	6	53	58	22	7	64
Higher Level	Mean	14	11	12	48	59	16	5	76
	s.d.	15	3	16	52	44	4	4	40

(*Times in minutes*)

Here again, considerable inter-school variability is apparent.

All other school sizes, '3–4 Class' and above

The difficulties of classification encountered with the smaller schools were fortunately absent with those larger.

It was decided at the outset to keep the categories I, J and S separate from each other and to explore the possibility of reporting, for each of these categories, a single mean and a single standard deviation for each of the several duties that would serve for all school sizes '3–4 class' and above. The method used will be illustrated for Category I, A duties.

For this category and duty there were 5 school sizes, '3–4', '5–6', '7–9', '10–13', and '14+', represented respectively by 4, 3, 10, 10, and 8 observations. A one-way analysis of variance was carried out between and within school sizes, with the results displayed in Table V.

TABLE V

Anova. Category I, A duties

Source	d.f.	SS	MS	F	
Between School Sizes	4	523·38	130·84	<1	NS
Within School Sizes	30	6483·02	216·10		
Total	34	7006·02	—		

The differences among School Size means are clearly not significant, so that it is sufficient to report a single mean time to represent all school sizes for this category and duty.

Since there were 3 categories and 8 duties, it was necessary to carry out 24 analyses of the type shown above. It is perhaps sufficient to report that in every case the same result was obtained—the differences among School Sizes were not significant.

This gratifying result made possible a considerable simplification in reporting. For each category and each duty, a single mean time and standard deviation (24 in all) was adequate for all school sizes of '3–4 class' and above. The results are presented in Table VI.

TABLE VI

School sizes '3-4 Class' and above. Duty time means and standard deviations

Duty	A		B		C by Observation		C by Interview	
Category	Mean	s.d.	Mean	s.d.	Mean	s.d.	Mean	s.d.
I	22	14	12	7	6	8	69	50
J	16	16	13	11	11	10	61	43
S	17	11	16	12	9	10	77	92

	Total C		D		E		S	
	Mean	s.d.	Mean	s.d.	Mean	s.d.	Mean	s.d.
I	74	53	20	11	9	6	84	51
J	72	45	24	24	7	5	72	56
S	85	93	15	10	8	12	49	52

(*Times in minutes*)

The discussion so far has dealt primarily with stratification by school size. It will be recalled that the sample was also stratified according to yearly stage. An examination of the data demonstrates that the only systematic variation in this respect is with regard to Supervision Duties. The means are 84 minutes of Supervision Duties for Infants, 72 for Junior and 49 for Senior. A one-way ANOVA was appropriate and gave the following results:

TABLE VII

Source	d.f.	SS	MS	F
Between levels (I, J, S)	2	24499·842	12249·921	4·394
Within levels	99	275983·972	2787·717	(2,99)
				Sig. at 5%
Total	101	300483·814	—	

There are therefore statistically significant differences among the I, J, S means quoted in the Final Report. Pursuing the matter further, and comparing individual means, we find the difference between

(i) I–and J–means to be not significant at 5 per cent;

(ii) I–and S–means to be significant beyond 5 per cent;

(iii) J–and S–means to be not significant at 5 per cent, but approaching significance.

IV. Discussion

The purpose of this study is to provide estimates of the times taken to perform certain duties in schools: estimates that will be useful to those concerned with the organisation of these duties. It would clearly be an advantage in planning if it could be said that duty A is likely to occupy x minutes and duty B to occupy y minutes and the two together (x + y) minutes. It would be helpful also if limits could be set within which the individual and total times are likely to lie.

It is useful to compare the situation with that in which we should find ourselves were we asked to estimate a child's IQ when we know nothing about him except that he is a member of a large population for which the mean IQ is 100. In this case the best estimate we can make of the child's IQ is 100. If in addition the population standard deviation is known and the distribution is normal, we can also set limits within which, at a pre-determined level of confidence, his IQ may be presumed to lie. For instance, supposing the population standard deviation to be 15, the 95 per cent confidence interval is from 70 to 130. In other words, if we have many such estimates to make, we shall be right 19 times out of 20 in the long run if we assert each time that a child's IQ lies within this range 70–130.

If for some reason we required the *sum* of two children's IQs under the conditions just stated, the best estimate of this sum would be $(100+100)=200$; the best estimate of the standard deviation of this sum $\sqrt{(15^2+15^2)}=21$ (approximately); and the 95 per cent confidence interval of this sum from 158 to 242 (approximately).

To a limited extent, the situation with the duty times resembles that described above. For each duty we do have a mean and a standard deviation. But there the resemblance ends. In the case of the child's IQ, we have population parameters on which to base our estimates. In the case of the duty times we have sample statistics only. We do not know the population values either for means or standard deviations. Furthermore, the sizes of the samples of individual duty times are not large enough to provide any indication of the nature of the population distribution. It would be hazardous to assume normality, or indeed any shape on which confidence intervals could be based that would be secure for a combination of duties such as would be performed in, for example, one day.

All that can be safely said is that the means and standard deviations reported earlier furnish some slight indications, based on small samples of duty times previously observed, of the sorts of times likely to be encountered in the future. If this unsatisfactorily vague statement were to be made more precise, a great deal of further experimental observation with much larger samples would be necessary.

It is doubtful, however, whether the results of such extra labour would be particularly helpful in practice. The fact is that for each duty the times are very variable. In one '1–class' school the time taken to perform the duty A is 2 minutes; in another it is 61 minutes. In one '3–4 class' school the time for duty E is 2 minutes; in another it is 46 minutes. In the light of this degree of variability, it is impossible to predict with any degree of precision how long a particular duty or combination of duties is likely to take on a particular day in a particular school. This conclusion, based on the evidence already available, cannot be altered by amplifying this evidence through further experimentation.

The practical implication of this variability is obvious. Planning for the short run (which in general is all that can be planned for) must be very flexible. If, for example, duties A, B and S are to be performed in a '3–4 class' school, the best estimate available of the total time required is $(17+16+49)=82$ minutes. But the planners must not be surprised if this combination of duties takes considerably less time, or considerably more.

C. Summary

(1) The raw data on which this Appendix is based were presented in different ways for different sizes of school so that different statistical treatments were necessary.

(2) For all duties, all school sizes, and all levels within school, the data showed considerable variability.

(3) The nature of the data was such that no firm estimates of the precision of mean times were possible.

(4) This is no great disadvantage, since even had such estimates of precision been possible, they would only have been helpful in long-run estimates of time taken. They would have been of little value in the short run situations arising in practice.

(5) Planning of duties must be sufficiently flexible to take account of the high degree of variability displayed in the data on which this Appendix is based; variability presumably typical of that to be encountered in the future.

'Simulated Days' for Various School Sizes and Auxiliary-Teacher Ratios

FIGURE I

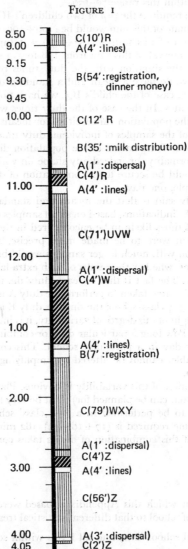

8.50 — C(10')R
9.00 — A(4' :lines)

9.15 —

9.30 — B(54':registration, dinner money)

9.45 —

10.00 — C(12' R

B(35' :milk distribution)

A(1' :dispersal)
C(4')R
11.00 — A(4' :lines)

C(71')UVW

12.00 —
A(1' :dispersal)
C(4')W

1.00 —
A(4' :lines)
B(7' :registration)

2.00 —
C(79')WXY

A(1' :dispersal)
C(4')Z
3.00 — A(4' :lines)

C(56')Z

4.00 — A(3' :dispersal)
4.05 — C(2')Z

KEY: 7 CLASS SCHOOL (CLASSES R U V W X Y Z) with teaching head.
RATIO: 1:7.

▭ : duties carried out on a Fixed Timetable.
▥ : duties carried out on a Flexible Timetable, or by a Sharing policy.
▨ : auxiliary's intervals and lunch break.

NOTE: (1) 12 hrs. 36 minutes of C and Supervision Duties are left undone on this basis.
(2) In the simulations, dinner duty (A) has not been included. If it is included then a greater degree of auxiliary assistance will be required.
(3) Class Z is the head teacher's class.

98

FIGURE 2

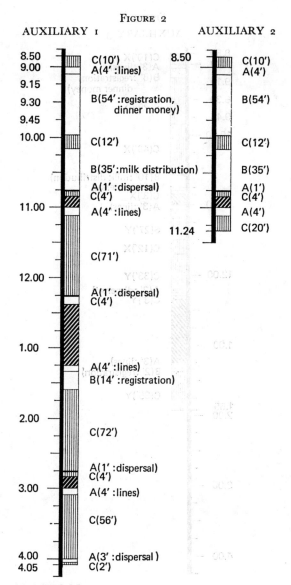

AUXILIARY 1   AUXILIARY 2

KEY: 14 CLASS SCHOOL.

      RATIO: 1:10.

      □ : duties carried out on a Fixed Timetable.

      ▥ : duties carried out on a Flexible Timetable, or using an On Call policy, or by a Sharing policy.

      ▨ : auxiliary's intervals and lunch hour.

AUX. 1, 2—Full-time auxiliaries.

AUX. 3—Part-time auxiliary.

NOTE: (1) 28 hrs. 35 minutes of C and Supervision Duties are left undone on this basis.

        (2) In the simulations, dinner duty (A) has not been included. If it is included then a greater degree of auxiliary assistance will be required.

        (3) 20 minutes C duties could be allocated to each class each day on this basis.

FIGURE 3

AUXILIARY 3

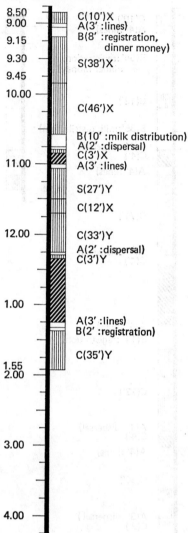

KEY: 2 CLASS SCHOOL (CLASSES X, Y).

RATIO: 1:3.

☐ : duties carried out on a Fixed Timetable.

▥ : duties carried out on a Flexible Timetable, or using an On Call policy, or by a Sharing policy.

▨ : auxiliary's intervals and lunch hour.

AUX. 1, 2 : Full-time auxiliaries.

AUX. 3 : Part-time auxiliary.

NOTE: (1) 1 hour 30 minutes of C and Supervision+8 of A Duties are left undone on this basis.

(2) In the simulations, dinner duty (A) has not been included. If it is included then a greater degree of auxiliary assistance will be required.

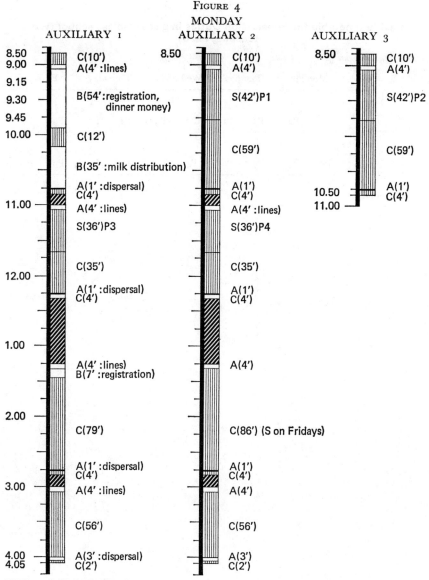

FIGURE 4
MONDAY

KEY: 7 CLASS SCHOOL (CLASSES P1, P2, P3, P4, P5, P6, P7).
RATIO: 1 : 3.

☐ : duties carried out on a Fixed Timetable.
▥ : duties carried out on a Flexible Timetable, or using an On Call policy, or by a Sharing policy.
▨ : auxiliary's intervals and lunch hour.

AUX. 1, 2 : Full-time auxiliaries.
AUX. 3 : Part-time auxiliary.

NOTE: (1) On Monday, 5 hours, 3 minutes of Supervision Duties are left undone on this basis.
(2) In the simulations, dinner duty (A) has not been included. If it is included then a greater degree of auxiliary assistance will be required.
(3) C could be kept constant at 77 minutes per class each day.
(4) Classes each day could have at least half the Supervision time required.

FIGURE 5

Possible timetable for Supervision Duties in a seven-class school (with teaching head)

Ratio 1 : 3. See Figure 4.

		Monday		Tuesday		Wednesday		Thursday		Friday	
Morning	{	P1	P2	P5	P1	P2	P3	P1	P2	P3	P4
	{	P3	P4	P7	P6	P4	P5	P6	P7	P5	P6
Afternoon										P7	

Analysis of an 'On Call' System for Supervision

(Prepared by Mr. N. L. Lawrie of the Department of Operational Research, University of Strathclyde)

1. The aim of the analysis has been to develop a model of the way teachers might use auxiliaries on an 'On Call' basis, and to use the model to predict properties of the system for any specified number of teachers and number of auxiliaries in particular, to predict what proportion of the time a teacher will get an auxiliary for a lesson for which she requests auxiliary assistance, and what proportion of the time auxiliaries will be free to carry out C duties.

2. The following detailed assumptions are made.

(1) Any auxiliary may assist any teacher. This is consistent with the assumption of shared auxiliaries providing that no auxiliary remains idle while a teacher with which that auxiliary is not normally associated requires auxiliary assistance.

(2) Teachers do not 'queue' for auxiliaries. They do not say they require an auxiliary and then defer the lesson for which the auxiliary help was required until an auxiliary becomes free. Rather, they help themselves.

(3) If an auxiliary is free when a teacher requires assistance with a lesson, that auxiliary goes to the classroom and remains with the teacher until the teacher's requirement ends. If no auxiliary is free, the teacher does without and begins her lesson, but may obtain assistance from an auxiliary for part of the lesson if one should become free during its course.

(4) It is assumed that each class in a school requires auxiliary assistance on average for the same proportion of each week. The evidence of the data collected is that, in general, Junior classes require less auxiliary time than Infant classes, and Senior classes less time than Junior.[1] It has, however, been shown [2] that

(1) Mean supervision times required for classes in schools with three or more teachers are:

> 84 minutes/day for Infant classes
> 72 minutes/day for Junior classes
> 49 minutes/day for Senior classes

and are in the ratio of 1·7:1·5:1·0

(2) Values of f and h (see Para. 4) were calculated for a range of m (number of teachers) and k (number of auxiliaries) and on the following assumptions about the ratio of time required per Infant class to time required per Junior class to time required per Senior class:

  (a) 1:1:1 (This is the simplifying assumption)
  (b) 2·25:2:1 (An assumption based on the results of the first wave)
  (c) 3:2:1 (Selected as an extreme estimate)

In every case, the different assumptions led to absolute differences in f and h of less than 1 per cent, the tendency of assumption (a) in relation to (b) and (c) being to overestimate f and to underestimate h.

the statistics defined in paragraph 4 of this Appendix are very little affected by making the simplifying assumption that each class in a school does require auxiliary assistance for the same proportion of each week, providing that the proportion taken is the mean of the proportions actually required by the various classes in the school.

(5) It is assumed that the expected number of calls for auxiliary assistance made in any short time interval depends only on and is proportional to the number of teachers not using an auxiliary during that interval.

This last assumption is perhaps less plausible than its predecessors. Suppose that auxiliaries are free to undertake Supervision between 11.30 a.m. and 12.30

103

p.m. each day. The assumption is that, if the same number of teachers were not using auxiliaries between 11.40 and 11.45 as between 12.20 and 12.25, the expected number of calls for auxiliaries would be the same in the two periods. This seems intuitively unlikely. Calls for auxiliary assistance would probably be less often made when only 5 or 10 minutes of working time remained.

Classrooms with auxiliaries have not, however, been observed in the Technological Study, and hence actual distributions of calls for auxiliaries and of times for which auxiliaries might be used are not available (the first of these distributions, at least, would be affected by the way auxiliaries were organised). It is only possible to make assumptions, more or less plausible, about them. For this reason, the results quoted in this Appendix should be regarded more as qualitative guides to what might happen if an 'On Call' system were used than as precise quantitative predictions.

Having made the above assumptions, it is now possible to examine a range of situations between:

(i) That in which teachers behave independently of one another. No teacher is less likely to call for an auxiliary at some point in time because all or most of the auxiliaries are with other teachers at that time. This situation occurs when the 'On Call' system is used, when there is no planning among teachers about when auxiliaries should be used, and when teachers do not know how many (if any) auxiliaries are free to help them at any time.

(ii) That in which teachers co-operate fully with one another. If there are enough auxiliaries to meet teachers' requirements, all of these will be met. In this situation, demands are spread out over the time available and the effect is in some respects similar to that of a Flexible Timetable.

3. Results of the analysis are given in graphs A to D and in Tables I and II. They have been calculated for combinations of values of four parameters, defined below.

    (1) m: the number of teachers in the school.
    (2) k: the number of auxiliaries in the school.
    (3) p: the proportion of the time for which each class requires auxiliary assistance for Supervision. P is defined as the ratio of 'time required per class per day for Supervision' to 'total time available per auxiliary per day for Supervision'. Thus, if the mean daily requirement per class for Supervision in a particular school were 120 minutes and the time per day each auxiliary had available after A, B and C type duties had been deducted were 180 minutes, P would be

$$P = 120/180 = 0.67$$

    (4) $\propto$: a measure of the degree of independence of teachers in their demands on auxiliaries. When $\propto = 1$, we have the situation where teachers behave independently of one another, and, as $\propto$ decreases, co-ordination between teachers increases until $\propto = 0$ which corresponds to complete co-ordination—in effect a Flexible Timetable. Results are now shown for values of $\propto$ other than 0 and 1.

4. Each of the four graphs show results for a different pair of values of m and k. For each graph, P is plotted along the horizontal axis, and the quantities plotted against P are:

    (1) the mean percentage of free time per server assuming teachers behave independently of one another (f).
    (2) the percentage of free time per server assuming full co-operation between teachers (f_1).
    (3) the mean percentage of the demand for auxiliary assistance actually met, given independent behaviour, i.e., given $\propto = 1$ (h).
    (4) the mean percentage of the demand actually met given full co-operation, i.e., given $\propto = 0$ (h_1).
    (5) the mean percentage of demands for an auxiliary met immediately, given $\propto = 1$ (j).

The pairs of values of m and k for which the graphs have been drawn are:

Graph A: m 7, k 1.
Graph B: m 7, k 2.
Graph C: m 14, k 3.
Graph D: m 14, k 4.

The meaning of the quantities plotted on these graphs is illustrated below.

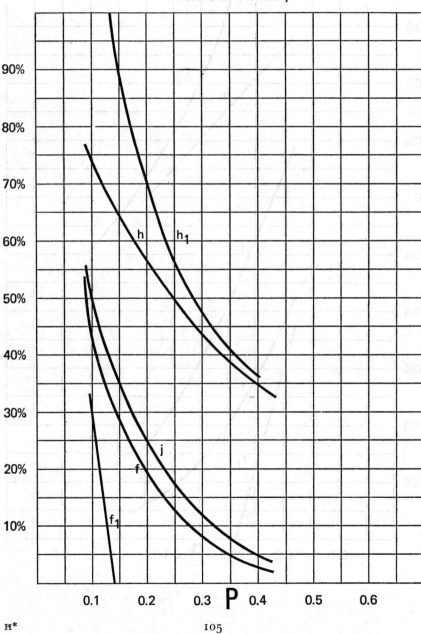

Graph A

7 Teachers: 1 Auxiliary

Graph B

7 Teachers: 2 Auxiliaries

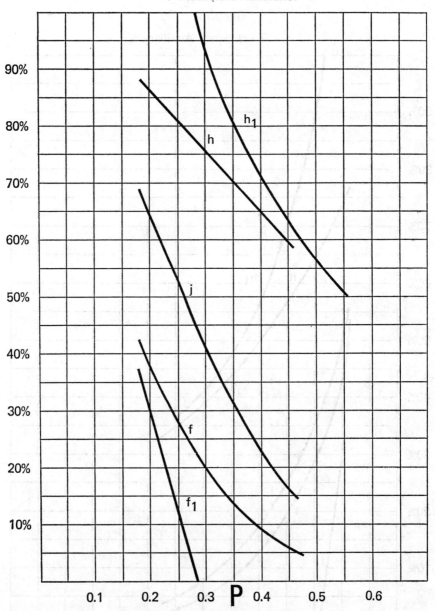

Graph C

14 Teachers: 3 Auxiliaries

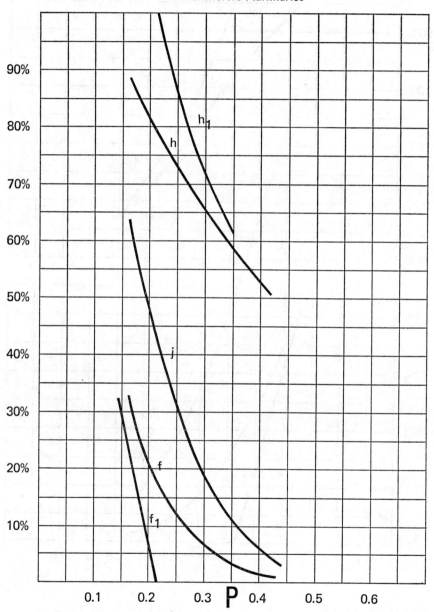

Graph D

14 Teachers: 4 Auxiliaries

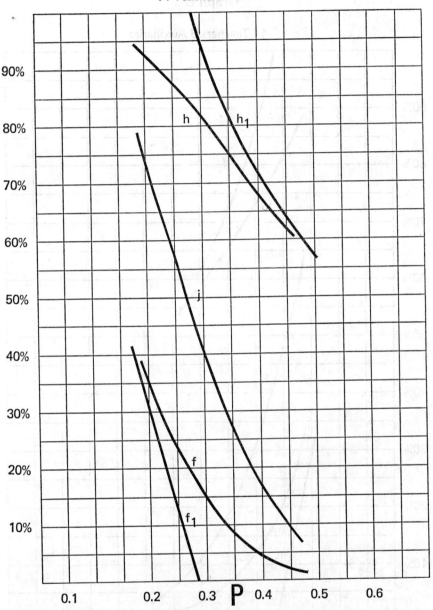

Use of the graphs

5. Suppose we are interested in the behaviour of an 'On Call' system for Supervision in a 7 teacher school where 2 auxiliaries are employed and where each has 160 minutes in each day available for Supervision Duties. Suppose that each class

requires an auxiliary for Supervision for an average of 60 minutes per day. Then $P = 60/160 = \cdot 375$ and from graph B we can read off the values

$$f \ = 11 \cdot 5\%$$
$$f_1 = 0\%$$
$$h = 67 \cdot 5\%$$
$$h_1 = 76\%$$
$$j \ = 28\%$$

Given that teachers behave independently of one another, each auxiliary would be free for $11 \cdot 5$ per cent on average of her time set aside for Supervision (160 mins.) i.e., for approximately 18 minutes per day, and each teacher would have the services of an auxiliary for $67 \cdot 5$ per cent of the time for which she needed one, i.e., for 40 minutes per day on average.

This may be compared with the values f_1 and h_1, which describe the Flexible Timetable system. Each day an average of 420 minutes of Supervision is required and only 320 minutes can be provided. Thus a Flexible Timetable could be devised to use all the auxiliaries' time ($f_1 = 0$) and would satisfy $(320/420) \times 100\% = 76\%$ ($= h_1$) of teachers' demands.

Notice that auxiliaries would be available throughout the entire lesson for only 28 per cent of the lessons for which teachers required them, given independence of behaviour. In the remaining 72 per cent of lessons, auxiliaries would either not be available at all or would arrive after the beginning of the lesson, remaining, however, to the end.

6. It should be noted that the curve of h_1 is horizontal at the value 100 per cent for values of P which are less than or equal to k/m, and then declines sharply. The curve of f_1 behaves in a converse fashion, dropping to 0 per cent at P equal to k/m and remaining at 0 per cent thereafter. Curves for f and h, for values of $\propto$ other than 1, lie between the curves of f and h shown and the curves of f_1 and h_1. The curve of j, for values of $\propto$ other than 1, lies above the curve j shown (for which $\propto = 1$).

Thus, as one would expect, utilisation of auxiliaries and the percentage of demand on auxiliaries met both improve as co-ordination between teachers increases. This co-ordination requires a communication system between teachers, although perhaps no more is required to achieve some improvement than informal discussion in the staff room. The improvement occurs because, with co-ordination, fewer demands for auxiliaries occur when all of them are busy.

Tables give more limited information than the graphs over a wider range of values of m (the number of teachers) and k (the number of auxiliaries). Results relate to the case where teachers behave independently of one another in their calls for auxiliary assistance, i.e., the case $\propto = 1$. Entries in each table are values of P which is as defined in para 3 above, and the more descriptive term 'level of service' denotes the quantity h defined in para 4. A level of service of 75 per cent means that, on average, a teacher will have auxiliary assistance for Supervision for 75 per cent of the time for which she requests such assistance.

The tables may be used in either of two ways.

(1) Having specified the number of teachers, and a value of P, one may look in the appropriate table for the least number of auxiliaries required to give the desired level of service. For example, for a 7 teacher school with $P = \cdot 50$, 3 auxiliaries will give a 75 per cent level of service. 4 are required to give a 90 per cent level of service.

(2) Having specified the number of teachers, the number of auxiliaries and the level of service required, one may look up the appropriate table to find the maximum value of P consistent with that level of service.

Although figures in each table are given to two decimal places, they should be used, as suggested earlier, more as a qualitative guide to what might happen with an 'On Call' system for Supervision than as an exact prediction.

TABLE I

Level of Service 75%

		k (number of auxiliaries)							
m (number of teachers)		1	2	3	4	5	6	7	8
	3	·28	·87	*					
	5	<·2	·45	·78	*	*			
	7	<·2	·30	·53	·74	>·9	*	*	
	9	<·2	·24	·40	·55	·73	·89	>·9	*
	12	<·2	<·2	·29	·41	·53	·65	·77	·89
	14	<·2	<·2	·24	·35	·45	·56	·66	·75

TABLE II

Level of Service 90%

		k (number of auxiliaries)							
m (number of teachers)		1	2	3	4	5	6	7	8
	3	<·2	·56	*					
	5	<·2	·25	·53	·84	*			
	7	<·2	<·2	·33	·53	·73	>·9	*	
	9	<·2	<·2	·25	·38	·53	·68	·83	>·9
	12	<·2	<·2	<·2	·27	·37	·48	·58	·70
	14	<·2	<·2	<·2	·22	·32	·40	·49	·58

Notes:

1. It is assumed that P does not exceed 1·0.
2. <·2 indicates a value of P less than 0·2.
3. >·9 indicates a value of P greater than 0·9.
4. Where * appears in a table, all values of P up to and including P=1·00 will give at least the level of service of that table.

Conclusions

7. (1) The Flexible Timetable apparently results in less free time for auxiliaries and a better service to teachers than the 'On Call' system. How real these benefits are is difficult to assess since they are obtained, in part at least, at the cost of a less flexible availability of auxiliaries. Auxiliaries may be available to a teacher for Supervision when they are not required, and may not be available (unless freed by another teacher) when they could in fact have been put to good use.

(2) When the value of P is large in relation to the ratio k/m, i.e., when demand for auxiliaries' time is considerably greater than the supply, f will be small and so will h, which cannot exceed k/mP. In this situation, most requests for an auxiliary would not be met and it would seem clearly better to adopt a Flexible Timetable in order to avoid frustration.

(3) When the value of P is less than k/m (this is unlikely to obtain in practice) or not much greater, the case for an 'On Call' system is defensible but not clearly stronger than for a Flexible Timetable. One final point worth noting is that if P is not much larger than k/m and an 'On Call' system is used, there will be an appreciable percentage of the time of auxiliaries set aside for Supervision free from requests for supervisory assistance. During this time, which will fluctuate from day to day, preparation could be done, providing that the results were not required in the short term. The time need not be wasted.

OLD FRIENDS AND NEW FANCIES

Sybil G. Brinton

When Georgiana Darcy and Colonel Robert Fitzwilliam break off their engagement, confessing that their mutual affection remains purely platonic, each is free to seek their spouse elsewhere. After seeing her perform in a concert, Robert warms to the beautiful and talented Mary Crawford — but Lady Catherine de Bourgh pays heed to spiteful tongues, and drives Mary from Rosings. Meanwhile, Kitty Bennet is staying in London as the protegee of a certain young lady named Emma Knightley. When introduced to charming naval officer William Price, younger brother of Fanny, Kitty swiftly loses her heart to him. But when William and Georgiana meet, will Kitty's dreams be shattered?

THE POWER OF DARKNESS

Edith Nesbit

A desirable semi-detached house harbours a dreadful scene. The strains of a funeral mass carry a warning to two young lovers. A bridegroom swears that death itself would not part him from his intended; another man's wife proves this true. Spirits of long-ago women reach out across the years, whilst a corpse refuses to leave its murderer alone. Waxworks appear so life-like, it's as if they are about to rise and walk — meanwhile, marble effigies in a village church are rumoured to do pre-cisely that. Welcome to that other world which beats a constant undercurrent beneath our own — the world which knows the power of darkness.

Organisational Questionnaire and Check-list

A considerable amount of information of a sociological and organisational nature was collected by Dr. Taylor during the Survey and it is hoped to issue this as a separate publication in the near future. Meanwhile, we include in this Appendix the organisational questionnaire and check-list which were used during the Survey.

FIGURE 1

Information on schools

—————————————————————————————School

1. School Roll: Please state your class designation and roll.

   P.1$_a$ P.1$_b$ ————————————
   P.2 ————————————
   P.3 ————————————
   P.4 ————————————
   P.5 ————————————
   P.6 ————————————
   P.7 ————————————
   Total

2. (a) Approximate age of school building(s) Years

   (b) Does the school accommodation include the following: Yes No

	Yes	No
General Purposes room	————	————
Gymnasium	————	————
Specialist Room (e.g., for art, sewing, etc.)	————	————
Dining Room (inside)	————	————
Toilets (inside)	————	————

3. Is the school equipped with the following audio-visual aids?

	Yes	No
Television	————	————
Radio	————	————
Tape Recorder	————	————
Projector (a) sound	————	————
(b) silent	————	————
(c) film strip	————	————
Record Player	————	————
Inter-communication system	————	————
Other	————	————

4. Please estimate the approximate percentages* of families in your school who live in the following types of houses:

Type	%
Private Houses/Flats	
Owner occupied	_____
Rented or Tied	_____
Crofts	_____
Council Houses/Flats	_____
Tenements	_____
Unknown	_____

5. Please estimate the approximate percentages* of Fathers or Heads of Household whose occupations fall into the following categories:

%

1. Professional and Administrative
   (i.e., Doctors, Lawyers, Teachers, Managers, Local Authority Officers) _____
2. Clerical (i.e., Clerks, Secretaries, Typists, Office Machine Operators) _____
3. Skilled (i.e., Market Gardeners, Postmen, Shop Assistants, Bus Drivers, Electricians) _____
4. Semi-skilled ⎫ (i.e., Agricultural Workers, Packers, Miners, Bus
   Unskilled ⎬ Conductors, etc.) _____
5. Unknown _____

6. Please state the average percentage of pupils receiving free meals during the past year. _____

7. Please state the percentage of pupils who have been referred to the School Psychological Service or Child Guidance Clinic during the past year. _____

8. Please state the percentage of pupils obtaining remedial help in the school during the past year. _____

9. If facilities are not available for remedial help at school, please estimate the percentage of pupils requiring remedial help. _____

10. Please state the numbers of full-time qualified staff:

	1965–66	1966–67
Present on 1st day of autumn term	_____	_____
Departed 2nd day autumn term to end of school year	_____	_____
Appointed 2nd day autumn term to end of school year	_____	_____

11. Please state the reasons for their departure.

12. Please state the number of unfilled vacancies short of establishment _____

13. Please state the attendance percentage for the primary department for the past year. _____

---

* Numbers were requested if the school was small.

The Schedule of Visits

The schedule of visits was designed to meet the requirements described in Chapter III (e.g., that as far as possible all school days should be equally represented and that sufficient time should be allowed for travel and for the processing of results). Except in the case of one-class schools both pairs of observers visited each school.

September (1967)	Monday, 18th	Shetland
	Tuesday, 19th	Travel
	Wednesday, 20th	Travel
	Thursday, 21st	Orkney
	Friday, 22nd	Travel
	Monday, 25th	Travel
	Tuesday, 26th	Ross and Cromarty
	Wednesday, 27th	Inverness-shire
		Argyll
	Thursday, 28th	Travel
	Friday, 29th	Ross and Cromarty
October	Monday, 2nd	Analysis
	Tuesday, 3rd	Travel
	Wednesday, 4th	Ross and Cromarty
	Thursday, 5th	Sutherland
	Friday, 6th	Travel
	Friday, 13th	Interview 2 schools Edinburgh
	Monday, 16th } Tuesday, 17th	Edinburgh
	Wednesday, 18th } Thursday, 19th	Analysis
	Friday, 20th } Monday, 23rd	Edinburgh
	Tuesday, 24th	Analysis
	Wednesday, 25th	Interview Clackmannanshire
	Thursday, 26th } Friday, 27th	Clackmannanshire
	Monday, 30th	Analysis
	Tuesday, 31st	Interview Fife
November	Wednesday, 1st } Thursday, 2nd	Fife
	Friday, 3rd	Analysis
	Monday, 6th	Interview 2 schools Aberdeen City
	Tuesday, 7th } Wednesday, 8th	Aberdeen City
	Thursday, 9th } Friday, 10th	Analysis
	Monday, 13th	Stirlingshire
	Tuesday, 14th	Analysis

	Wednesday, 15th Thursday, 16th	Aberdeen City
	Friday, 17th	Analysis
	Monday, 20th	Interview Moray and Nairn
	Tuesday, 21st Wednesday, 22nd	Moray and Nairn
	Thursday, 23rd Friday, 24th	Analysis
	Monday, 27th	Ayrshire and Angus
	Tuesday, 28th	Analysis
	Wednesday, 29th	Interview Ayrshire
DECEMBER	Thursday, 30th Friday, 1st	Ayrshire
	Monday, 4th	Analysis
	Tuesday, 5th	Interview Wigtownshire
	Wednesday, 6th Thursday, 7th	Wigtownshire
	Friday, 8th	Analysis
	Monday, 11th	Interview 2 schools Dunbartonshire
	Tuesday, 12th Wednesday, 13th	Dunbartonshire
	Thursday, 14th Friday, 15th	Analysis
	Monday, 18th Tuesday, 19th	Dunbartonshire
	Wednesday, 20th Thursday, 21st	Analysis
1968		
JANUARY	Monday, 8th	Interview Berwickshire
	Tuesday, 9th Wednesday, 10th	Berwickshire
	Thursday, 11th Friday, 12th	Analysis
	Monday, 15th	Lanarkshire
	Tuesday, 16th	Analysis
	Wednesday, 17th	Interview Renfrewshire
	Thursday, 18th Friday, 19th	Renfrewshire
	Monday, 22nd	Analysis
	Tuesday, 23rd	Interview 2 schools Glasgow
	Wednesday, 24th Thursday, 25th	Glasgow
	Friday, 26th	Analysis
	Monday, 29th	Interview Angus
	Tuesday, 30th Wednesday, 31st	Angus
FEBRUARY	Thursday, 1st Friday, 2nd	Analysis
	Monday, 5th Tuesday, 6th	Glasgow
	Wednesday, 7th	Analysis
	Thursday, 8th	Interview 2 schools Lanarkshire

	Friday, 9th }	Lanarkshire
	Monday, 12th }	
	Tuesday, 13th }	Analysis
	Wednesday, 14th }	
	Thursday, 15th	Interview 2 schools Glasgow
	Friday, 16th }	Lanarkshire
	Monday, 19th }	
	Tuesday, 20th }	Analysis
	Wednesday, 21st }	
	Thursday, 22nd }	Glasgow
	Friday, 23rd }	
	Monday, 26th }	Analysis
	Tuesday, 27th }	
	Wednesday, 28th	Interview Angus
MARCH	Thursday, 29th }	Angus
	Friday, 1st }	
	Monday, 4th }	Analysis
	Tuesday, 5th }	
	Wednesday, 6th	Interview Angus
	Thursday, 7th }	Angus
	Friday, 8th }	
	Monday, 11th	Analysis
	Tuesday, 12th	Interview Renfrewshire
	Wednesday, 13th }	Renfrewshire
	Thursday, 14th }	
	Friday, 15th	Analysis
	Monday, 18th }	Glasgow
	Tuesday, 19th }	
	Wednesday, 20th }	Analysis
	Thursday, 21st }	
	Friday, 22nd	Lanarkshire
	Monday, 25th	Analysis
	Tuesday, 26th	Interview Perthshire
	Wednesday, 27th }	Perthshire
	Thursday, 28th }	

Printed in Scotland by Her Majesty's Stationery Office Press, Edinburgh.
Dd. 244625/2597 K4 9/70 (7650)